Puzzles of the Body

Studies on Themes and Motifs in Literature

Horst S. Daemmrich
General Editor

Vol. 10

PETER LANG
New York • Washington, D.C./Baltimore • San Francisco
Bern • Frankfurt am Main • Berlin • Vienna • Paris

David Kenosian

Puzzles of the Body

The Labyrinth in Kafka's *Prozeß*, Hesse's *Steppenwolf*, and Mann's *Zauberberg*

PETER LANG
New York • Washington, D.C./Baltimore • San Francisco
Bern • Frankfurt am Main • Berlin • Vienna • Paris

Library of Congress Cataloging-in-Publication Data

Kenosian, David.
  Puzzles of the body : the labyrinth in Kafka's Prozess, Hesse's
Steppenwolf, and Mann's Zauberberg/ David Kenosian.
      p.   cm. — (Studies on themes and motifs in literature; vol. 10)
  Includes bibliographical references and index.
  1. German fiction—20th century—History and criticism. 2. Labyrinths
in literature. 3. Quests in literature. I. Title. II. Series.
PT772.K45   833'.9120915—dc20   93-44803
ISBN 0-8204-2426-9
ISSN 1056-3970

Die Deutsche Bibliothek-CIP-Einheitsaufnahme

Kenosian, David:
Puzzles of the body : the labyrinth in Kafka's Prozess, Hesse's
Steppenwolf, and Mann's Zauberberg/ David Kenosian. - New York;
Washington, D.C./Baltimore; San Francisco; Bern; Frankfurt am Main;
Berlin; Vienna; Paris : Lang.
  (Studies on themes and motifs in literature; Vol. 10)
  ISBN 0-8204-2426-9
NE: GT

The paper in this book meets the guidelines for permanence and durability
of the Committee on Production Guidelines for Book Longevity of the
Council of Library Resources.

© 1995 Peter Lang Publishing, Inc., New York

Printed in the United States of America.

ACKNOWLEDGMENTS

I wish to thank Kathryn Hellerstein and Cynthia Appl for their kind help in preparing the final manuscript. With their assistance I was able to make this study more readable. Any mistakes and awkward passages remaining are my fault alone. Special thanks go to Professor Horst S. Daemmrich who supervised this project when I first wrote it as a dissertation. I cannot imagine how I would have written the revised version without his help, support, and encouragement.

Contents

CHAPTER 1

Introduction

Theseus, the much celebrated hero of classical mythology, undoubtedly felt a dizzying rush of excitement when he finally saw the light at the exit of the labyrinth. Outside, Ariadne waited, hoping her beloved Theseus would emerge victorious from his deadly struggle. Inside the dark, forbidding labyrinth lay the slain Minotaur, a ferocious, hideous beast that inspired awe and horror among Athenians. Every nine years, King Minos of Crete had demanded human tribute from Athens: a group of young Athenians were delivered to Crete and had to enter the labyrinth, a confusing edifice with a number of paths that came to a dead end. Only one path led to the center and back out. The Minotaur savagely killed all those who lost their way in the labyrinth. By vanquishing the Minotaur, Theseus gave his young countrymen new life and, in so doing, assured himself a place among the heroes of Athens.

Indeed, the story of his duel in the labyrinth became a frequently told one in classical mythology. The history of the labyrinth does not, however, stop there. The labyrinth has been an enduring and widely recognized motif and design in the Western cultural tradition. Throughout its rich and varied history, it has been associated with such binary oppositions as light-darkness, understanding-confusion, and life-death. The mythological labyrinth at Crete may well have been associated with another opposition: spirit-nature.[1] A variation of this opposition is the mind-body polarity, a conceptual pair that has figured prominently in ontological discussions. Humanity does not belong exclusively to the realm of nature or of the spirit but to both simultaneously. To the extent that we are physically present in the world as empirical beings, we are part of the natural order. However, our reasoning ability distinguishes us from the rest of nature. The Minotaur literally embodies the mysterious, animal-like forces in humanity. The Minotaur has the body of a man, but instead of having a human head, the symbol of the intellect, he has the head of a bull (von Brück 304). Except for his head, the Minotaur is identical in nearly every way to Theseus. The myth of Theseus should then be read in terms of the mind-body polarity. Theseus represents humanity in its intellectual confrontation with its own corporality. In other words, upon entering the labyrinth, Theseus faces the puzzle of human embodiment. His triumph symbolically gives primacy to mind over body, and thus corresponds to a central figure in Western thinking.

In von Brück's reading, the myth of the Cretan labyrinth is an early interpretation of an issue that would occupy Western philosophers for centuries to come. I do not maintain that all labyrinths over time relate to the mind-body issue. On the contrary, the myth of the labyrinth, like most other myths, lost its hermeneutical function by the modern period. In the eighteenth century, an age generally hostile towards mythology, the mind-body polarity was the subject of systematic philosophical inquiry. According to Terry Eagleton,[2] issues relating to the body took on great significance in aesthetics. Idealist aesthetics[3] is a discourse whose main concern is mediating between the universal laws of reason and a broadly defined realm of the body: the individual's somatic drives, emotions, affectations, and sensory experiences (Eagleton 15). Within this framework, philosophers begin constructing new models of the subject. In contradistinction to its predecessors, the bourgeois subject internalizes the laws of reason. The autonomous subject gives itself the laws of reason to which it freely submits its sentient domain. Kant, for example, situates reason in the atemporal moral self which regulates the temporal empirical self. In the Kantian subject reason structures the subject's perceptions and shapes its moral life. In general, philosophers in the 18th century saw the development of autonomous, moral subjects as an integral part of a larger process: the progression of civilization towards the goal of perfection.

During the eighteenth century, the labyrinth appeared much less frequently in works of literature than in previous centuries.[4] This is hardly surprising since the signifier of confusion was surely out of place in an age when thinkers sought to establish a rational order in the world. But by the late nineteenth century, the motif of the labyrinth enjoyed a resurgence in American and European literature.[5] The city labyrinth captures the confusion of modern industrial society, which, ironically, is a product of Enlightenment reason. The process of modernization caused profound intellectual disorientation for individuals and societies since there was no historical precedent for modern social forms.[6] Modernism, the aesthetic response to this radical change, can be defined as the art of the rapidly industrializing world, a world of advanced technology, urbanization, secularization, and mass forms of social life.[7] The component parts of the city labyrinth can be seen as a causal explanation of this cultural confusion. The city captures the forces of modernization (cause) which triggers the cultural confusion (effect) signified by the labyrinth. The motif of the labyrinth is then a cipher for the cultural crisis of the early twentieth century, the intellectual confusion of individuals and societies whose rapid development challenged traditional forms of thought.

Few discussions of the modernist labyrinth analyze the motif in German literature.[8] Yet modernization caused disorientation in Germany as well as the other economically advanced European nations. In the German context, the rise of the modern metropolis touched off a crisis among young writers beginning in the 1880s.[9] Many felt that they could no longer represent the world in the same way as their predecessors the Realists. The Realists have, as Russell Berman argues,[10] aesthetic assumptions that reach back to the

Enlightenment: the possibility of rational communication, the priority of reasonable rules, and exchanges of meaning among equals (55). For much of the nineteenth century, writers emphasize the moral or ethical ties that bonded the individual to the world (the universal). Goethe's *Wilhelm Meister* had provided writers with a model *Bildungsroman*. In the novel of development, a young protagonist undergoes a process of total personality development with the ultimate purpose of becoming a useful member of society. The protagonist would encounter representatives from different walks of life who would give him insights into the nature of the world. The protagonist's process of self-realization is aided by the counsel of a few influential individuals who help him learn and enhance his process of inner growth. In this idealized notion of *Bildung*, the ethical appears, according to Terry Eagleton, as a custom, a law of the spirit which converts the first nature of appetites and desires into a second or spiritual one which will become customary to the subject (Eagleton 22). But after Germany had become a modern industrial nation in the late nineteenth century, writers no longer believed that they could represent individual development in society in the same way as Goethe and the Realists had done. Similarly, Berman maintains that a number of Wilhelmine intellectuals thought that the modernization and bureaucratization of social life snuffs out any chance of a genuine ethical community. Thus, for German modernist writers, urbanization was a main cause of the crisis of the Classical-Romantic tradition.

This study examines three texts, Kafka's *Prozeß*,[11] Hesse's *Steppenwolf*,[12] and Thomas Mann's *Zauberberg*,[13] in which the motif of the labyrinth functions as a signifier of the cultural crisis. All three questers, Josef K., Harry Haller, and Hans Castorp, traverse the labyrinth to find a meaningful way of being in the world. They must orient themselves in a world whose traditions and value systems are breaking down. Two questers, Josef K. in *Der Prozeß* and Harry Haller in *Der Steppenwolf*, try to find their way in city labyrinths. Castorp, to be sure, moves not through a city but rather the sanatorium labyrinth. But the Berghof sanatorium must be considered in light of the Venice labyrinth in Mann's *Der Tod in Venedig*, the text to which *Der Zauberberg* was conceived as a counterpart.

These three texts give new insights into this crisis since the motif of the labyrinth is more than a metaphor for a confusing world. The configurations which support the motif of the labyrinth furnish information on a crucial aspect of the cultural crisis: the growing uncertainty concerning the mind-body relationship. Thus, the use of the motif of the labyrinth in these works represents a return to the myth of Theseus. In *Der Prozeß*, *Der Steppenwolf* and *Der Zauberberg*, corporality plays a twofold role in the figures' quest to find the meaning of life. First, the questers' progress in the labyrinth hinges on their way of relating to the body. Second, they must develop an interpretation of life in terms of corporality. On this basis, I propose an allegorical reading of the labyrinth: the questers' movement in the labyrinth represents their progress in finding a way of understanding the human individual as an embodied subject. The figures gain understanding of their own corporal being by reflecting on death, the negation of their empirical self.

These writers, along with leading philosophers and intellectuals, were participating in a decades long process of rethinking the German cultural tradition, a tradition which was shaped by German Idealism. To be sure, German Idealism is not primarily concerned with the body, although there are, as Eagleton shows, traces of the body in the discussion of ethics, perception and politics. But in the course of the nineteenth century, corporality becomes an increasingly important topic.

Kant's legacy had a decisive influence on Schopenhauer, who at the same time succeeded in giving Kantian philosophy a new direction. For Kant, the thing-in-itself is the sublime object in the noumenal realm. Schopenhauer[14] essentially replaces the thing-in-itself with the will. But the will is not confined to the noumenal realm: according to Schopenhauer's concept of the principium individuationis, all entities in the (phenomenal) world are manifestations of the will in space and time. While these representations can be material in nature, they appear to us only as representations. As far as human individuals are concerned, the only entity given both as an objectification of the will and as a representation is the body. Like another material object, the human body is spatial and temporal and, as such, it is "given in intelligent perception as representation" (Schopenhauer I: 100). Implicitly, the body, like the will, serves as a bridge between the noumenal and the phenomenal. After asserting that the body is a condition of knowing one's own will, Schopenhauer actually postulates the identity of body and will (I: 102).

Schopenhauer marks an important stage in the development of German Idealism, for his philosophy elevates the status of the body. Nietzsche, Schopenhauer's enthusiastic pupil, goes one step further. In *The Gay Science*,[15] Nietzsche argues that philosophy is an interpretation, or more accurately, a misinterpretation of the body:

> Behind the highest value judgments that have hitherto guided the history of thought, there are concealed misunderstandings of the physical constitution...All those bold insanities of metaphysics, especially answers to the question about the *value* of existence, may always be considered first of all as the symptoms of certain bodies. (36)

Nietzsche's own philosophical enterprise is to a great extent founded on the

attempt to rethink corporality.[16]   In *The Will to Power*,[17] he redefines the
subject on the basis of the body:

> The body and physiology are the starting point: why? -We gain the
> correct idea of the nature of our subject-unity, namely as regents at
> the head of a communality (not as "souls" or "life forces"), also of the
> dependence of these regents upon the ruled and of an order of rank
> and division of labor as the conditions that make possible the whole
> and its parts. (271)

In this quote, Nietzsche effectively repeats the logic of idealist aesthetics
in one crucial respect: the body is presented as a metonymy of social relations.
Similarly, the later Nietzsche reads culture in terms of the body:

> For Nietzsche...culture as a text is a discourse wherein we must
> discover its method of functioning...and also its meaning, to the extent
> that this text refers back to what it does not contain: life, the body,
> as its principle and its referent. (Blondel 79)

The notion of corporality is present in Nietzsche's analysis of the
Apollonian and the Dionysian, the conceptual pairs used to interpret Greek
culture in *The Birth of Tragedy*.[18]   The Apollonian and the Dionysian are
contrasting art worlds analogous to physiological phenomena. The Apollonian
is conceived as the world of dreams, the Dionysian as that of intoxication (33).
Apollo, the god of light, is the ruler of the inner world of fantasy which
Nietzsche sees as the analogue of the soothsaying faculty and, more
importantly, of the arts.   Nietzsche sees Apollo as the divine image of
Schopenhauer's principium individuationis (36). The Dionysian, on the other
hand, is exemplified by the ecstasy which overcomes this principle. Under the
influence of Dionysian emotions, individuals celebrate the primordial unity of
humanity with nature and among individuals (37).   The feeling of unity was
often realized by "sexual licentiousness" (39), or in other words, the sexual
union of separate bodies. It is certainly fitting that the celebration of the unity
with nature was marked by eros since the body is associated with nature in
German Idealism.

Eros, a fundamental aspect of corporality, plays a key role in the process
of self-realization of K., Haller, and Castorp. Death, another crucial aspect
of this process, is also a result of human embodiment. Death is of course the
central issue in the existential phenomenology of Martin Heidegger, who
began to rethink ontological questions around the time when *Der Prozeß*, *Der
Steppenwolf*, and *Der Zauberberg* were written. The thinking of the early
Heidegger can be seen as the first systematic philosophical response to

corporality.[19]   Heidegger grounds his concept of morality and interpretation
in temporality, the time of the body.   Dasein (human existence) relates
interpretatively to its own being, and this being is primarily corporal (Eagleton
304).[20]   Indeed, the notion of the body is implied in the idea of the spatiality
of Dasein (Heidegger, *BT* 148).   The body not only occupies space but also
has its own time.   Dasein's time is limited by death, the cause of its existential
guilt.   Temporality can therefore be understood as a time frame imposed by
the body.

At the same time, temporality is the basis of self-understanding.   Within
its temporal horizon, Dasein must project itself onto its future possibilities,
above all death.   By projecting itself onto its own future possibilities, Dasein
interprets its own being.   Dasein's projection in time is the common element
in Heidegger's concepts of morality and interpretation.   In fact, Heidegger's
analysis of temporality and morality in *Kant and the Problem of Metaphysics*[21]
comes close to undermining one of the tenets of the idealist tradition, the
timeless moral self. According to Kant, individuals can begin to achieve self-
realization by respecting the moral law that we should not treat others as a
means to an end.[22]   Rather, we should respect this law by freely subjecting
ourselves to it.   Heidegger, however, locates respect in the empirical realm by
defining it as a feeling (Sherover 164).   Heidegger further describes respect
as Being's "authentic Being-its-self" (Heidegger, *KPM* 109).   Authenticity is
possible only if Dasein projects itself onto its death, the cause of its guilt.
Thus, we must face our guilt if we are to respect the law.

In Heidegger's philosophy, there is no longer an atemporal self which
imposes moral laws on the bodily domain.   Individuals can find the moral law
by confronting death, the negation of their empirical being.   Similarly, the
quester figures in the three texts must have an encounter with death in the
labyrinth in order to understand life in terms of corporality.   In the following
chapters, I pursue a thematic analysis to trace the variations of the motif of
the labyrinth and to show the different function of corporality in each work.
I base my understanding of thematology on the work of Horst Daemmrich.
Like Daemmrich, I see themes as fundamental, transcultural aspects of human
existence and experience.   They are concepts supported by motifs, the smallest
signifying units in a text.   This thematic study will demonstrate how the
component parts of the labyrinth furnish information on the quester figures'
relationship to the body.

In chapter two, I will provide a brief history of the labyrinth.   The starting
point of the analysis will be the labyrinth in the ancient world, the source of
the Greek myth from which the authors draw.   The analysis shows that the
functions of the labyrinth in Crete and ancient Greece are congruent with the
body-mind polarity.   As an edifice, the labyrinth is an intellectual challenge,
a test of the questers' orientation.   The labyrinth was also used in rites to

celebrate the cycles of nature. In these rituals, the way into the labyrinth leads to darkness and death, while the way out leads to light and new life. In the Western literary tradition, the individual constituent elements of the labyrinth, the motifs of the path, light, and darkness, frequently signify figures' existential orientation. The motif of the path gives information on figures' direction in life, and the motifs of light and darkness furnish information on their level of self- and world-understanding. My analysis is not limited to labyrinths in the ancient world. I will briefly trace the historical development of the labyrinth in order to examine some of the different kinds of labyrinths that have evolved, labyrinths whose constituent elements are imbricated with various discourses. I will focus primarliy on those labyrinths which correspond to variations of the motif in the three texts.   In chapters 3 through 5, I argue that Kafka's *Prozeß*, Hesse's *Steppenwolf*, and Mann's *Zauberberg* concern more than just the search for the meaning of life. In all three texts, the figures are challenged to understand life in terms of corporality. Indeed, the motif of darkness appears in conjunction with lust and the fear of death, which, as I indicated in the discussion of Heidegger, can be understood as a response to one's own embodiment. If the figures cannot intellectually confront the mortality of their empirical selves, they get lost in the darkness of the labyrinth. If, however, the quester figures are prepared to have an encounter with death, they successfully orient themselves and move towards the light, a metaphor for their new understanding of life.   Through the figures' process of self-realization, the authors present alternative models of individual and societal development: they deploy the Classical-Romantic tradition against philistine thinking and instrumental reason; invoke the need for a spiritualized community to replace reified social relations; and show how channelling the unconscious drives can regenerate the individual.

Chapter 3 concerns Josef K.'s quest for understanding in Kafka's *Prozeß*. K. enters the city labyrinth to get advice on his trial. In this chapter, I propose a new reading of K.'s case: the trial reflects the breakdown of idealist aesthetics in that there is no longer a pre-existing ethical code which the court enforces. Rather, defendants must find the moral law to govern their own empirical being. Underlying the configurations of the text is a dialectical conception of corporality. Figures with a material relationship to the body are doomed to fail in their trial. But figures with an intellectual relationship to the body can potentially discover the moral law by reflecting on death, the negation of their own empirical being. In this respect, Kafka's *Prozeß* bears a striking similarity to Heidegger's early philosophy. In *Der Prozeß* defendants must write a moral interpretation of their lives based on this kind of anticipatory reflection. The burden on defendants is especially great since they must transcend the interpretative horizon of the peremptory and arbitrary court to which the interpretations are presented. K. moves throughout the city to find help in writing his defense. Thus, his movement in the labyrinth is an allegory for his progress in interpreting his life. In the end, his blundering on the same darkened dead end reveals that he fails to reflect critically on his reified way of being.

Chapter 4 examines Harry Haller's quest for the meaning of life in Hesse's *Steppenwolf*. Like K., Haller moves through a city labyrinth in search of the meaning of life, but the figure of Haller differs significantly from that of K. In contrast to the materialistic K., Haller is a writer who reflects on politics and Germany's Classical-Romantic tradition with which he identifies. On this basis, I offer a new reading of Haller: he is an allegory of German *Geist* and his disorientation in the city represents the crisis of the German cultural tradition in the modern world. While Haller, like K., continually moves to dark spaces in the labyrinth, Haller eventually succeeds in reversing his direction and gaining self- and world-understanding. The key to Haller's process of intellectual growth is the sensuous (bodily) experiences he has with women. On an allegorical plane, this is to be read as *Geist* striving to achieve harmony with *Natur*. Further, these sensuous experiences enable him to enter the realm of vision in his mind including the Magic Theater, which is represented as a labyrinth. Of the three texts in this study, Hesse's *Steppenwolf* is the only one in which the quester's psyche is represented as a labyrinth. But *Der Steppenwolf* does share this configuration with another work from the 1920s. Gustav Hocke[23] argues that in Joyce's *Ulysses*, both Dublin and Bloom's unconscious are represented as labyrinths. Since both the city in *Der Steppenwolf* and Haller's mind are labyrinths, his exploration of drives, repressed memories, and cultural imprints in the labyrinth of his mind is implicitly a model for cultural renewal.

In chapter 5, I present an analysis of Hans Castorp's movement through the sanatorium labyrinth in Mann's *Zauberberg*. Castorp is the sole figure who does not enter a city labyrinth. The sanatorium must be considered as a variation of the Venice labyrinth in *Der Tod in Venedig*. *Der Zauberberg* was originally intended to be the humoristic counterpart to *Der Tod in Venedig*, and, more crucially, both the sanatorium and Venice are places of disease which signify the inexorable decay of nineteenth-century bourgeois culture. In *Der Zauberberg*, the patients' mindless pursuit of bodily pleasures keeps them confined to the world of Berghof. By contrast, Castorp begins to learn about life by studying the body in a variety of fields. Further, Castorp traverses the sanatorium labyrinth to observe how the patients confront their own mortality. The figure of Castorp is more than just an individual who seeks answers to life's mysteries. Like the figure of Haller, Castorp is an allegorical figure who represents Germany. Along these lines, the contrasting patterns of light and darkness, constitutive elements of the labyrinth, appear in conjunction with the Western European Enlightenment and the German

Romantic tradition. In the text, both traditions are linked to specific attitudes towards corporality. Castorp develops a new interpretation on ontological and cultural issues on his ascent of the mountain, a movement which follows the same course as ancient dances which celebrate Theseus' success in the labyrinth. In the end, Castorp cannot use his insights to help Germany. Instead, he becomes a soldier on the battlefield which is actually the recurrence of the sanatorium labyrinth in a transfigured form. The war labyrinth is Mann's unique variation of the motif, and clearly establishes a causal link between the cultural crisis, as signified by the sanatorium, and the political catastrophe. Castorp's likely death in the war raises the question of whether his insights can provide a solution to the cultural crisis.

CHAPTER 2

A Brief History of the Labyrinth

2.1 Introduction

The labyrinth has been an enduring motif in the Western cultural tradition. Because the history of the labyrinth is both long and complex, I can give only a brief outline of its historical development. In spite of the complicated evolution of the motif over time, two general remarks can be made about the labyrinth. First, the labyrinth furnishes the reader with information about the world in which the questers live, for it is closely connected to the dominant cultural realm of a given society. From the royal dynasties of Egypt to the medieval church and the cities of the nineteenth and twentieth centuries, the labyrinth is associated with the value center of a society. It expresses ideas about the beliefs and attitudes of that culture toward life. Hence, the motif of the labyrinth provides the reader with vital information about the relationship of the individual to the world. The motif gives information about the world and about the ability of questers to find their way in that world.

Second, the labyrinth represents a challenge of orientation to those who enter, usually questers. They must successfully find orientation in a confusing space in which they could easily become lost. They frequently face choices at crossroads. Most scholars agree that the principle elements of the labyrinth include a variety of paths, intersections, and the possibility of error. Umberto Eco[1] goes even one step further to show how these characteristics are common to three major types of labyrinths. While Eco provides a clear analysis of the basic structural features of the labyrinth, he does not go into its historical development. I will expand on his study by pointing out how the particular types of labyrinths were used in different historical periods.

The first is the labyrinth of Crete which is supposed to have housed the Minotaur. Eco argues that the Cretan labyrinth is structurally a skein, a unicursal spiral pattern, and that Theseus had no choice but to reach the center (80), a view I do not fully share. In fact, Penelope Reed Doob asserts that myths of a multicursal Cretan labyrinth existed as early as Homer.[2] The second type of labyrinth which Eco discusses is the maze, or *Irrgarten*, which first appeared in the late Middle Ages. This kind of labyrinth does not have a Minotaur at its center; it is therefore a puzzle without the danger associated with the mythological labyrinths. The maze offers a choice of paths, some of which are dead ends. Some alternative paths end at a point at which one must reverse direction while others lead to new paths. Only one path leads to the way out (Eco 81).

The third type of labyrinth is a net. It has two main features: all points can be connected with one another; and even if the connections are not yet designed, they are conceivable and designable (Eco 81). The network labyrinth has an almost unlimited variety of alternative paths and lacks a center. To illustrate this type, Eco examines the concept of the rhizome as developed by Deleuze and Guattari. Eco identifies two unique features of the rhizome:

> No one can provide a global description of the whole rhizome; not only because its structure changes through time; moreover, in a structure in which every node can be connected with every other node, there is also the possibility of contradictory inferences. (Eco 81-82)

It is also a structure with no outside: the observer can only examine it from the inside.

Eco's analysis provides a useful starting point for a brief discussion of the history of the labyrinth. I will focus primarily on the historical background of the Cretan labyrinth for two reasons. The authors, especially Hesse and Mann, use elements of Greek mythology in the texts interpreted in this study. Furthermore, the myth of Theseus is the best known version of the labyrinth in Western civilization.

2.2 The Labyrinth in the Ancient World

In the Western tradition, the labyrinth has been an enduring symbol which C. N. Deedes[3] traces back to the ancient Egyptians. Originally, it was an architectural structure designed to defend the burial site of the royal family. In the ancient world the labyrinth was associated with the mysteries of life. It was the place where the king-god was resurrected from the dead and the fertility of nature was celebrated. In time it was associated with the god Osiris. Eventually, Osiris was not only identified with the dead king but also with his temple and the pyramid. This close relationship may have served as the basis for the yearly religious festivals held at Abydos. The myth of Osiris was presented as a drama, with other members of the royal family and priests playing key roles.

The labyrinth and Osirian drama continued to occupy an important place in Egyptian religious life into the Middle Kingdom (2160 - 1788 B. C.) when Cretan craftsmen were employed by the pharaoh, especially during the reign of Amenemhet III and his predecessors (2000 B. C.). Amenemhet III built an enormous temple, known as the labyrinth, next to his pyramid in the Fayoum (Deedes 16). Pliny discussed the temple as having baffling, winding ways, columns of white Parian marble, and doors which suddenly slammed shut (Deedes 17). According to Pliny, this building served as a model for Daedalus, who supposedly was the architect of the famous Cretan labyrinth at Knossos. As we will see, Pliny's report bears a striking resemblance to the description of the sanatorium in Mann's *Zauberberg*.

The palace at Knossos was both a religious and administrative center of Crete. There, as in Egypt, the monarch was a king-god. According to R. F. Willetts,[4] the king was supposedly the offspring of the Mother Goddess, the chief deity in the Cretan religion. She was a "huntress and goddess of sports, armed or presiding over ritual dancing with apparent dominion over mountain, sky, earth and sea, over life and death; she is at once a household goddess, a palace goddess, vegetation and fertility goddess, a mother and a maid" (Willetts 120).

Yet another parallel between Crete and Egypt is the central role of the bull in the rituals conducted at the labyrinth. Didorus, Pliny, and Herodotus even believed that the Cretans received their mysteries from Egypt; the mysteries of Isis being the same as those of Demeter and the mysteries of Osiris being those of Dionysus.[5] In fact, later rituals suggest that bulls were sacrificed to the Mother Goddess so that she might guarantee a rich yield of crops. The Cretan ritual closely resembles the Osirian mystery rites: a bull was sacrificed to a king-god who was identified with a god of fertility. In addition, some kind of resurrection play was performed. Over time, the Greeks adopted the bull cult from the Cretans (MacKenzie 187).

But for the Athenians, the bull cult and labyrinth had much different meanings, as evidenced by the myth of Theseus. Here, for the first time, the labyrinth is not a symbol of resurrection and life but rather of menace and death. The story of Theseus and Ariadne after the slaying of the Minotaur expands the field of meaning of the labyrinth. Before returning to Athens, they stopped at Naxos and Delos. There are several versions of Ariadne's fate: Theseus left her while she slept at Delos, and she died there; or

Dionysus took her as his bride at Naxos. At Delos, the group performed a dance, the Crane Dance, which Daedalus had taught Theseus and which imitated the windings of the labyrinth. The eighteenth book of the *Iliad* describes the dance.

Ariadne's mythological nature helps shed some light on the Delian Dance. Based on the Theseus myth, she is associated with Artemis and Aphrodite. The rituals for the goddess of vegetation of Naxos may hold the key to the identity of Ariadne. At Naxos, she had two festivals which were perhaps part of the same festival. One was a festival of rejoicing in honor of Ariadne as a bride of Dionysus. The other was a festival of mourning for Ariadne who dies at Naxos after she was left by Theseus (Willetts 121).

Though he agrees that the death of Ariadne is a vital part of the dance, Karoly Kerenyi[6] differs as to which goddess was to be honored. Kerenyi examines the dances at Delos which were held in honor of Aphrodite, who, he argues, represents a "higher form" of Ariadne:

> Diese Form setzt den Tod der Ariadne voraus...so daß wir hier zugleich von einer Persephonegestalt reden dürfen: von einer Göttin deren Idee-dem Wesen der Persephone entsprechend-Leben und Tod vereinigt. (Kerenyi 38)

The dance in Ariadne's honor represents the triumph over death:

> Die Begehung fand in der Nacht statt. Die in Delos gefundenen inschriftlichen Rechnungen erwähnen Seile und Lichter, die bei den Tänzen des Aphroditefestes gebraucht wurden. Beides-Seil und Fackelschein-erinnert sehr an Persophonesfeste. (Kerenyi 38-39)

The dancer held a rope, Ariadne's string, while moving in a spiral to the left, the direction of death. Upon reaching the mid-point, the dancer was supposed to turn around and move in the opposite direction, the direction of birth (Kerenyi 39). The celebration of birth and death points to other deities, such as Artemis, Britomaris, and Persephone. Kerenyi's last observation on the affinity of the Delian dances to one another helps clarify Ariadne's complex nature: she was probably identified with both Aphrodite and Artemis.

From the time of the Old Kingdom in Egypt to that of Minos, the labyrinth was a cult center which represented a dark mysterious place of transformation: the labyrinth was identified with the triumph of the afterlife over death, and the rise of a deity from the underworld to the heaven. In addition, it was associated with gods of fertility and vegetation, whose resurrection symbolized the regeneration of nature as it revives from its winter dormancy.

Upon being taken up in Greek mythology, the meaning of the labyrinth changed to a place of death. Thus, emerging from the labyrinth signalled not transformation but survival over hostile forces. Still, an essential aspect of the labyrinth remained: a quester figure, Theseus, successfully enters and leaves the labyrinth after vanquishing a bull figure. Finally, the dance depicts the winding course of the labyrinth. It not only symbolizes Theseus' path but also the cyclical nature of life: the return of vegetation and the triumph of birth over death.

The motif of the labyrinth found continued use in the Roman Empire. The Romans devised both unicursal and multicursal labyrinths, and sometimes depicted the latter in mosaics (Doob 42). Since labyrinths frequently appear in the medieval art of Western Europe, it appears that the Romans spread the image of the labyrinths throughout the empire in Europe.

2.3 Medieval Labyrinths

The motif of the labyrinth occurs in a staggering number of works in the Middle Ages. Doob, in her thorough and brilliant study, focuses on the multicursal labyrinth, which consists of a series of choices at intersections. Each choice is a test which requires thought or a decision. On this basis, she argues that the labyrinth is a sign of aesthetic complexity and moral or intellectual difficulty (Doob 46).

The labyrinth appears in aesthetic and religious texts alike. The motif occurs in Chaucer's *Legend of Ariadne* and in Boccaccio's *Genealogy of the Gods*. In Langland's *Piers Plowman*, the world is represented as a moral labyrinth (Doob 147-149). Specifically, the world is a confusing place in which the errors (incorrect choices) are sins. A version of the moral labyrinth appears in Petrarch's *Liber sine Domine*. There, Avignon and Babylon are both depicted as sinful labyrinths (Doob 158). Doob argues that Dante's hell is a labyrinth: hell has many circles and paths but it lacks a defined path which leads through the circles to the center. The whole point of hell is thus its inextricability (Doob 282).

The labyrinth also occurs in a number of religious texts. The religious labyrinth frequently has one of two conflicting meanings. It can represent sublime, divine artistry of God's creation or a spiritually dangerous world from which God alone can rescue humanity. Gregory of Nazianus sees God as a Daedalus figure who created a magnificent, though complex world (Doob 67). But the negative conception of the labyrinth is far more common. Gregory of Nyssa presents the labyrinth as everlasting death, from which only Christ-Theseus can save us (Doob 73). In his *Contra Symmachum*, Prudentius maintains that Christian Dogma is the Ariadne's thread which can save individuals from heresy and paganism (Doob 76). One of the more unusual uses of the labyrinth was the dance on the mosaic labyrinth at the cathedral at Auxerre. Clergymen performed the dance, which celebrated Christ-Theseus saving religious individuals from the labyrinth of hell through the mysteries of Easter (Doob 125).

Doob fails to discuss one particular sinful medieval labyrinth which bears a striking resemblance to the Berghof sanatorium in Mann's *Zauberberg*. I am referring to the Jericho labyrinth. In a large number of manuscripts, the city Jericho is described as a labyrinth or as being in the center of a labyrinth. Evidence of this association of Jericho with a labyrinth covers a period of roughly a thousand years not only in Roman-Catholic Western Europe but also in Greek-Orthodox Byzantium and in the Jewish-Syrian area.[7] One illustrated manuscript from the twelfth century depicts a Cretan (circular) labyrinth with a Latin inscription:

> The city of Jericho was shaped like the crescent of the moon....(T)he text and the illustration contain the puzzling association Jericho/moon and Jericho/labyrinth. The...statement is easily explained: in Hebrew the words for Jericho (yeriho) and moon (Yareh) have the same root, Yrh....Hence the name Jericho means 'city of the moon'-a meaning which can be found first in the writings of the Father of the Church, Hieronymus (about 400 A. D.) and was later adopted by the Medieval encyclopedists, Isidor Bishop of Seville...and Hrabanus Maurus, Abbot of Fulda and Archbishop of Mainz.... (Kern 19-20)

Some Jericho-labyrinths have the city itself in the center surrounded by seven walls (Kern 20). The seven circles correspond to Roman representations of the labyrinth.

It is uncertain how the connection between Jericho and the labyrinth took place. The answer may lie in the similarity between the Cretan and the Jericho labyrinth in the Jewish tradition. In the Roman Catholic and Greek Orthodox churches of the Middle Ages, the aforementioned medieval authors referred to changing phases of the moon as representing the inconsistency of the world (Kern 22). Like the labyrinth, Jericho, the moon city, is a symbol of a sinful world.

2.4 Labyrinths of the Seventeenth and Eighteenth centuries

The labyrinth appears frequently in the seventeenth century in a number of the forms identified by Doob. One popular use of the labyrinth was the maze-like gardens which were constructed at courts. These were not menacing places like the Cretan labyrinth. Rather, these gardens were puzzles to amuse the royal residents of the courts. In a similar fashion, literary labyrinths were used as linguistic puzzles. Gustav Hocke argues that a Roman mannerist poet Optantianus Portyrius wrote labyrinth poems ("Buchstabenlabyrinthe") out of rows of letters. Hocke goes further in asserting that the labyrinth was the symbol of Roman and Florentine Mannerism in the seventeenth century (19-20).

At the same time, the labyrinth served as a cipher for the confusing process of understanding the world. The seventeenth century was an age which witnessed the European discovery of vast segments of the globe, an historical development which helped shatter older notions of the world. Gerald Gillespie[8] has given us new insights into the development of the labyrinth from Dante to the end of the seventeenth century. He states that in the Age of Discovery, exploring the mysteries of the human mind and the newly discovered parts of the world can be represented as movement through the labyrinth. As an example, he cites Lohenstein's poem "Aufschrift eines Labyrinths" (Gillespie 80-81). The labyrinth that we discover externally in the maze of the world corresponds to the one we find "internally in the maze...of the human brain" (Gillespie 80). This is, to my knowledge, the first time the human mind was represented as a labyrinth. This particular variation of the labyrinth does not reappear until the twentieth century in Joyce's *Ulysses* and Hesse's *Steppenwolf*. The use of the motif of the labyrinth can no doubt be attributed to the widespread notion of the confusing, paradoxical nature of the world in the seventeenth century. Not surprisingly, the labyrinth appears much less frequently during the Enlightenment in the following century. In the eighteenth century, there was a widely held belief that order could be given to the world through the power of reason. Eco describes one of the more interesting innovations of the labyrinth which occurred in the eighteenth century, the rhizome labyrinth. The French encyclopedist D'Alembert applies the labyrinth to his project of organizing fields of knowledge. The labyrinth is a cipher for the complexity of the network of knowledge which lacks a center (Eco 83).

It is significant that D'Alembert's labyrinth represents a challenge to reason. This notion underlies the city labyrinths of the nineteenth and twentieth centuries. For D'Alembert, this challenge can be mastered if the philosopher assumes the proper vantage point, one from which the individual can look down upon the whole of the labyrinth. This implies that individuals can position themselves outside the labyrinth in order to orient themselves; but this very possibility is questioned in the literary labyrinths of the twentieth century.

2.5 Modernist Literary Labyrinths

Throughout its evolution, the labyrinth has displayed one enduring characteristic: it is a challenge of orientation. At the same time, the field of meaning of the labyrinth shows remarkable diversity. The labyrinth symbolizes the underworld in antiquity, the sinful secular world in the Middle Ages, the human mind in the poetry of Lohenstein, and epistemological structures in D'Alembert. In their analyses of the literary labyrinths of the nineteenth and twentieth centuries, Manfred Schmeling and Wendy Faris[9] expand on these findings. They both strive to trace the transition of the labyrinth from a specific topos to a structural principle in texts. Faris explores the labyrinth in Joyce's *Ulysses*, Robbe-Grillet's *Dans le Labyrinthe*, and in the works of Borges. According to Faris, the modern literary labyrinth becomes an icon, a sign whose physical qualities corresponds to those of its referent. The iconic embodiment of the labyrinth duplicates the form of the labyrinth in the design of the text: the placement of words, sentences and ideas (Faris 5).[10] One structural feature she cites is the multiple occurrences of events, which correspond to the series of choices which questers face in the multicursal labyrinth. This in fact does apply to the stages of the questers' movements in Kafka's *Prozeß*, Hesse's *Steppenwolf*, and Mann's *Zauberberg*.

In Faris' reading, the confusion of the figures in the text is an allegory for the confusion of readers who struggle to make sense of the text. But Faris weakens the force of her argument by asserting that nearly all confusing and structurally complex literature is labyrinthine. She even goes so far as to say that in postmodernism, the labyrinth is a sign of language itself (Faris 164). This conclusion is, however, not given adequate substantiation. Schmeling, on the other, hand does not give his reading of the labyrinth adequate historical grounding. He fails to say whether the architectural labyrinth represents preexisting structures of the mind, or whether psychoanalysts have used the idea of the labyrinth as an explanatory tool. Thus, lacking a historical framework, Schmeling cannot distinguish the labyrinth from other complex, bewildering structures in literature. In the end, he also implies that much post-war fiction has a labyrinthine structure.

I would argue that the labyrinth can be both a place (topos) and a structure. In either case, the labyrinth consists of a series of choices among different possibilities, and this is a crucial point that can easily be overlooked. It is vital not to lose sight of the fact that the constituent elements of the labyrinth give information on particular aspects of human experience in a given historical period. The difference between D'Alembert's labyrinth and the one at Auxerre is ample evidence of that. For this reason, the motif of the labyrinth structures the fields of meaning of those aspects of human experience on which the constituent elements of the labyrinth provide information. I will now shift the focus to Kafka's *Prozeß*, in which the motif of the labyrinth structures a discourse of the body.

CHAPTER 3

Labyrinths of the Law in Kafka's *Prozeß*

3.1 Introduction

Labyrinthine is an appropriate term for Kafka's writing, which almost seems designed to leave the reader in utter confusion. Deleuze and Guattari[1] argue that the underground home of the creature in "Der Bau" is a labyrinth. The burrow is a rhizome-labyrinth, a structure with multiple, intersecting paths, and is a paradigm for Kafka's texts as a whole. "Only the principle of multiple entrances, prevents the introduction of the enemy, the Signifier, and those attempts to interpret a work that is actually open to experimentation" (13). Hermann Pongs[2] uses the term labyrinthine as a cipher for the intellectual disorientation of modern civilization which, according to Pongs, has lost its ethical moorings. Pongs does not, however, undertake a systematic analysis of the city-labyrinth in Kafka's *Prozeß*.[3] I disagree with Schmeling's argument that the labyrinth in Kafka's *Schloß* and *Prozeß* is not a topos but rather a metaphor for the confusing world in the texts (175). On the contrary, the fact that the city, an obvious topos, and the court system share the same labyrinthine structure indicates that the court system is plagued by the same crisis that plagues the larger culture: the tension between the sensuous realm of the body and ethical laws. Moreover, an analysis of the labyrinth in all of its variations (city labyrinth and hermeneutical labyrinth) gives the reader a new understanding of Kafka's view of the cultural crisis of the early twentieth century: the inability to explain the modern world with existing cultural codes.

In *Der Prozeß* the motif of the labyrinth, in all of its variations, links this cultural crisis with Josef K.'s search for the meaning of life. The constituent elements of the labyrinth, the motifs of the path, light, and darkness, furnish the reader with information about the quester's existential orientation (Daemmrich 214-215, 340-342). Further, these motifs appear in conjunction with the themes of eros, death, and dread, which, as the analysis of Nietzsche and Heidegger showed, are responses to corporality. Thus, the labyrinth represents a test of the quester's ability to understand life in terms of corporality.

In addition, the motifs of light and darkness signify K.'s understanding of the process of interpreting life. In order to prepare a defense, defendants must put their reflection on their life experiences in writing. The defense is then submitted to the court, a massive organization for processing texts (the files of defendants). K. moves through the city to seek advice for his case; he has conversations with Huld and Titorelli who explain various strategies for writing a defense. The motifs of light and darkness which occur during these discussions indicate whether K. understands how to produce a written interpretation of his life. If the two functions of the theme of the labyrinth are taken together, then the labyrinth can clearly be seen as a challenge to write an interpretation of life in terms of corporality.

A fundamental aspect of corporality, eros, has long drawn the attention of critics. Some existentialist critics such as Wilhelm Emrich[4] and Walter Sokel[5] argue that K.'s erotic desire is a symptom of his inauthentic existence. Horst Turk[6] was one of the first to examine *Der Prozeß* in terms of Lacan's theory of desire. Turk reads the novel as a virtual textbook example of Lacan's theory: the subject, K. must obey the law of the father, i.e., he must repress his sexual desire. In his interpretation of *Das Schloß*, Ulf Eisele[7] maintains that the castle and the village are a linguistic world which operate by the laws of desire. For this reason, all the figures operate as tropes in a realm of ambiguities and shifting meaning. Likewise, Avital Ronell[8] points out that interpretation has erotic overtones in *Das Schloß*; neither the desire for understanding nor erotic desire is fulfilled in the text. Ronell's valuable study raises the issue of eros and the text; but few critics, with the exception of Gerhard Neumann,[9] have examined the function of the body per se. Neumann argues that Kafka strives to conceive of a new relationship between the body and the linguistic sign in order as the grounding of a new culture. "Es ist der Wille, eine *andere* Kultur zu denken als die bestehende, anstelle der 'Wahrheit der zirkulierenden Zeichen' die 'Wahrheit des stummen Körpers,' der weder Lizenz noch Tabu kennt, zur Grundlage der Kunst zu machen" (185).

I agree with Neumann's conclusion that Kafka is concerned with rethinking culture with respect to the body. I would argue further that new insights on the possibilities and limitations of this project can be gained by examining not just the body but also corporality, i.e., the figure's relationship towards empirical being, an issue which encompasses death and eros. Eros and death determine the outcome of the task facing Josef K.: developing new cultural relations by writing an interpretation of his existence as an embodied subject.

I share the view of poststructuralist critics that Kafka's works problematize traditional notions of literature.[10] Clayton Koelb[11] and Henry Sussman[12] argue that Kafka's texts self-reflexively thematize their own resistance to interpretative closure. Stanley Corngold[13] on the other hand examines the question of writing and argues that Josef K.'s relation to the law mirrors Kafka's relationship to writing literary texts. K. mistakenly thinks that he can defend himself on the basis of his personal experience, a grave error since Kafka himself believes that "the relations with others constituting ethical experience cannot supply writing with a model for its own discipline" (Corngold 242). This implies a near absolute barrier between the textual and the existential, to use Sussman's terms (104). This barrier is breached, however, by Ronell and Rainer Nägele,[14] who have explored the issue of interpretative desire.

I would go even further by arguing that for the accused in *Der Prozeß*, corporality is the decisive factor in *writing* an interpretation of life. The relationship of the accused to corporality is crucial for two reasons. First, the figures' desire must be channelled towards interpreting life in terms of the body. In this way, embodied subjects are called upon to produce a textual self-reflection. Second, the body is, in a sense, the object of writing since defendants must present their interpretation which redefines the universal law of reason. In Kantian thinking, autonomous subjects must freely impose moral laws on their own bodily domain (Eagleton 78). There is in this a similarity to Lacan's thinking: a decisive stage in the development of the subject is the rerouting of desire away from the body of the mother into the symbolic realm of language and culture. But in *Der Prozeß*, the only way to give a moral interpretation of empirical being is to reflect on death, the negation of empirical being.

The difficulty of producing a textual reflection on one's own embodiment is symptomatic of a larger cultural crisis which is captured by the city labyrinth. *Der Prozeß* takes place in a modern European city. Historically, the theme of the city gives information on the state of civilization; then the city-labyrinth signifies cultural confusion. Further, the representation of a modern city as a labyrinth indicates that the cultural disorientation has come about through the process of modernization. Indeed, the city-labyrinth in the literature of the late nineteenth and early twentieth centuries frequently signifies the confusion of individuals about the societal institutions which give order and meaning to civilization (Daemmrich 206-207). The crisis of the cultural tradition makes reflection on civilization problematic. This in turn is reflected by the spectrum of contradictory interpretations of "Vor dem Gesetz." Significantly, it is a parable of a man who cannot find the law. The cultural crisis is signified by the city-labyrinth. I will further show that the interpretations of the parable "Vor dem Gesetz" form a hermeneutical labyrinth which bears a remarkable resemblance to Humberto Eco's model of semiotics (or culture). The fact that the labyrinth recurs on the plane of interpretation is a sign that the cultural crisis has shaped the civilization's methods of interpreting itself. K.'s movement in the labyrinth can be seen as a cipher for his progress in producing a written interpretation of life in terms of corporality. Like the man from the country in "Vor dem Gesetz," K. is on a quest for the law, the ethical basis of life.

Finding the ethical basis for living is closely linked to finding the right intellectual food for the body. The law must mediate between the intellect and the body. To paraphrase Emrich, this corresponds to the function of food in "Forschungen eines Hundes": the food which the determined dog tries to find is supposed to bring about the "Synthese irdischer und unirdischer Existenz" (Emrich 157). Food involves the notion of the body since it fulfills a somatic need. In other texts by Kafka, bodily transformation is caused by not finding the right food. In "Die Verwandlung" Gregor Samsa becomes a human in the body of an insect. In "Der Hungerkünstler" the body of the hunger artist is reduced to a virtual skeleton. Significantly, both figures suffer from a somatic need, hunger. Metaphorically, food can be seen as the ethical basis for life, as the non-material sustenance which is provided through culture. For in the end, Gregor Samsa discovers that music is the nourishment he has been lacking. The hunger artist, however, cannot identify the right food. This failure suggests that the cultural crisis may be caused by the inability of civilization to regulate the sensuous realm of the body. Such an interpretation would be supported by the practices of the authorities in "In der Strafkolonie." There, laws are literally inscribed into the flesh of disobedient soldiers. The implications of "In der Strafkolonie" point to the societal dimension of K.'s quest for the law. The model of the subject in idealist aesthetics serves as a basis of social relations; the universal law of reason is supposed to govern the sensuous particulars, human individuals. It would seem that the only alternatives are the collapse of a repressive social order or the aggressive application of laws to the body. By contrast, no one in *Der Prozeß* can actually say what the law is (Deleuze and Guattari 43). Thus, the challenge for defendants is to *find* the moral law to govern their own empirical being.

The law and guilt must be seen in terms of the dialectically structured discourse of the body in *Der Prozeß*. Individuals can have either an intellectual or material orientation towards the body. This is reflected by the dual signification of the term "Gericht," which can mean either a meal or court, an organization for enforcing ethical norms. In a sense, both terms pertain to bodily incompleteness: food clearly fulfills a somatic need; and in idealist aesthetics, mysterious drives of the body are threats to ethical laws. Guilt is far more than failing to uncover one's true self as Emrich maintains (292). Guilt in *Der Prozeß* bears a striking similarity to Heidegger's notion of guilt in *Being and Time*. The individual is by nature guilty, i.e., mortal and incomplete; guilt impels the individual to find the law, the ethical basis of life. If individuals have a material relationship to the body, they will not gain the understanding needed to find the law. Consequently, they will remain in the darkness of the labyrinth and be convicted. If, on the other hand, individuals have an intellectual relationship the body, they can obtain the knowledge to discover the ethical law.

An intellectual relationship to being presupposes reflection on death, the negation of the empirical self. This can be inferred from a close reading of the parable "Vor dem Gesetz." The configurations in the parable give crucial insights into the meaning of the motifs of the path, light, darkness, and death which support the motif of the labyrinth in *Der Prozeß*. In the parable, all have their own unique path, a traditional metaphor for life. The man from the country has the desire to understand his situation; he continually requests permission to enter and pesters the guard with questions. The guard comments on his hunger for knowledge with the remark "Du bist unersättlich" (Kafka, *Der Prozeß* 257). Hunger clearly represents the desire for an ethical basis in life, in other words, the law. There is apparently food, or the law, but like Gregor Samsa and the hunger artist, the man from the country does not know how to search for it. The man does not gain any understanding, as signified by the light from inside, until he knows that he will soon die. Only then does he reflect on his past experiences. Hence, in order to interpret their lives, individuals must anticipate their own death. This clearly echoes Heidegger's views on Dasein. If Heidegger's concept of temporality is applied to the guard's statements, a new explanation emerges for why the guard answers the man's questions about entering with the laconic response "Jetzt nicht." Thus, Derrida[15] is right in saying that understanding is deferred but not indefinitely. Rather, understanding is possible through anticipatory self-projections onto death. Congruent with this, Kafka asserts elsewhere that the wish to die is a sign of growing understanding ("Erkenntnis").[16] According to Gustav Janouch, Kafka himself believed that confronting death enriches our lives.[17]

There is no doubt that the parable is a baffling text, even for the interpreters in the court. It seems that the man from the country is frustrated by a willful court functionary. Yet the guard gives a substantive response when the man asks the final question. Hence, the first significant exchange of meaning occurs when the man confronts death. Exchange, in the broadest sense of the term, is a central aspect of interpretation in *Der Prozeß*. K., like other defendants, must have discussions with a variety of interlocutors including court officials to make sense of the trial. According to Eagleton, the laws of reason in idealist aesthetics were thought to regulate linguistic exchanges. Eagleton asserts that

> ...the law of reason is a mechanism which, like the commodity, effects formally equal exchanges between isolated individual subjects, erasing the difference of their needs and desires in its homogenizing injunctions. (83)

The reference to material exchanges is a source of tension which emerges when K. has discussions with women and later tries to write his petition.
Since Kafka's works problematize the notion of a firmly established, pre-given law, the very basis of linguistic exchange is in question. Exchange is, as Berman shows, a central category of German aesthetic theory in the nineteenth century. Hence, Kafka's *Prozeß* problematizes language as well as the literary tradition.

I would argue that the exchange of meaning is not an a priori impossibility. Rather, linguistic exchanges are possible if the interlocutors are willing to help each other. According to Emrich, individual seekers in Kafka's texts must engage the viewpoints of all others if they are to transcend their limited perspective and understand being (45). In "Forschungen eines Hundes,"[18] the lone dog initially believes that he is dependent on the help of all dogs to find the right food. Significantly, the first question the dog addresses concerns the source of his sustenance: "Woher nimmt die Erde die Nahrung für uns?" (Kafka, *Beschreibung* 257). The commitment to help find the sustenance must go so far that the dogs in "Forschungen eines Hundes" are willing to sacrifice their lives. Thus, the dogs, like the man from the country in "Vor dem Gesetz," are dependent on others to gain understanding. There are in *Der Prozeß* a number of individuals such as Huld, Titorelli, and Frau Grubach who are willing to help him. But K. must also engage others in the court who seem to thwart the defendant at every turn. This, and the aggressive sexuality of some court members typify the abusive power relations in the court. Although such members of the court do not themselves understand life, they are expected to process the defendants' interpretation of life. The defendant must then transcend the interpretative horizon of court officials. In both cases, the encounter with death is the precondition of obtaining information about the meaning of existence. Kafka actually discussed a similar state of affairs with respect to his own readers. For Kafka, writing about the death of a figure gives his own life meaning, but leaves his readers in utter confusion:

> An allen diesen guten und stark überzeugenden Stellen handelt es sich immer darum, daß jemand stirbt, daß es ihm sehr schwer wird...und daß das für den Leser, wenigstens meiner Meinung nach, rührend wird. Für mich aber, der ich glaube, auf dem Sterbebett zufrieden sein zu können, sind solche Schilderungen im geheimen ein Spiel, ich freue mich ja in dem Sterbenden zu sterben, nütze daher mit Berechnung die auf den Tod gesammelte Aufmerksamkeit des Lesers aus, bin bei viel klarerem Verstande als er....[19]

For Josef K., death has a twofold function in producing a written interpretation of life. Reflecting on death enables defendants to have substantive exchanges with helpers and to go beyond the epistemological boundaries of the court's interpreters. K.'s progress in his quest to find the law will hinge on whether he can develop an intellectual relationship to the body by anticipating death.

3.2 City Labyrinth

In the Western literary tradition, the theme of the city frequently captures the state of the depicted civilization. Since the city is shaped by the organization of society, the representation of the city furnishes the reader with information on the intellectual life (*Geist*) of the depicted society. From the mid-nineteenth century on, European writers use desolate cityscapes to represent the ills of modern industrial society. Irving Howe[20] and Volker Klotz[21] maintain that Charles Dickens, whom Kafka greatly admired, was one of the first European writer to depict the horrors of modern urban life in his later novels. According to Diana Festa-McCormick,[22] European literature subsequently abounds with images of dark, foggy streets; dirty, seedy slums; and bleak, gray cityscapes. From the mid nineteenth century on, cities frequently embody the ills of a sick society; for instance, in Zola's *L'Assommoir* and D'Annunzio's *Child of Pleasure* (Festa-McCormick 46, 51). Hartwig Isernhagen[23] argues that the city in the fiction of the late nineteenth century has a deadly effect on nature and humanity alike. In his reading, the image of the city

> ...impliziert eine Selbstverlust des Individuums in der Masse, der mit der Entwicklung einer Eigendynamik und Eigengesetzlichkeit des Lebens in der Stadt...einhergeht. Es ist ein Verlust von *Natur* (Naturgegebenem), der sich auch in der Denaturierung aller Werte äußert.... (Isernhagen 82)

Isernhagen links the city to the destruction of nature and ethical values. These are the two essential components of aesthetics which, in Eagleton's terms, is a discourse of the body. By implication, the increasingly materialistic orientation of modern society causes a breakdown in the dominant cultural code. As a result, the relationship of some figures is shaped by the materialistic values of society. Klotz argues that in Dickens' *Hard Times*, the body of the figures is reduced to a commodity (153). Additionally, the personality of figures becomes a commodity as well; it increasingly seems to be a collection of elements with different exchange values.[24] In section 3.6, I will show that K. also treats the body of female figures as a commodity.

The bleak, dark streets and neighborhoods in texts are integral parts of the city labyrinth. But there is an additional aspect of the city labyrinth which distinguishes it from other representations of the modern city. According to Howe, figures in nineteenth century fiction can still escape from the city to the country. In twentieth century fiction, the city becomes a maze from which the protagonist cannot escape (Howe 41). Along these lines, the quester in a labyrinth risks getting lost in a confusing enclosed space. Questers, in fact, face two possible fates in the labyrinth: becoming entrapped or reaching freedom. Their challenge of orientation in the city labyrinth represents the challenge to find intellectual orientation in the modern world.

The characteristics of the modern city in general and the city-labyrinth in particular both apply to the nameless city in *Der Prozeß*. The city is replete with examples of the ills besetting modern society. There are at least two slums (near the homes of Titorelli and Huld) which have decrepit housing. In the apartment building on Julius Street, the residents live in squalid overcrowded apartments. In addition, nature is virtually absent from the city.[25] Indeed, the culture cannot even represent nature in art; Titorelli presents paintings of barren landscapes. To apply Isernhagen's terms, the disharmony between nature and spirit (civilization) is a sign that the culture's ethical codes are breaking down.

Further, the city can be seen as a labyrinthine maze. It is a dark, confusing, menacing space filled with a number of intersecting paths. Throughout the text, the city is continually shrouded in fog, clouds, or darkness. In the gloomy city, K. makes his way to distant buildings in strange neighborhoods. To do so, he must continually choose the right streets (paths) at intersections. The paths of the labyrinth are the streets which are filled with monotone, decrepit housing. Since, however, spaces in the city reflect each other, orientation is extremely difficult. In fact, the repetition of spaces and situations is a frequently occurring technique that can best be understood as mirroring. Mirroring is consonant with the structural principle of the labyrinth in that spaces and paths appear to be identical, thereby confusing the quester. Indeed, the two poor neighborhoods at opposite ends of the city (Huld's and Titorelli's) appear quite similar. On Julius Street even the houses mirror each other; there is not even a house number that might distinguish one house from the others.

But in this labyrinth there is no center. All of K.'s paths take him to court facilities which, as Titorelli tells him, can be found in the attic of every apartment building. Nevertheless, no one knows where the real administrative center of the court is. The chapter "Das Haus," in which Titorelli takes him to the main chancellery, was removed from the novel. Consequently, there is no center in the labyrinth. Since the court is spread out through the city, the court too has a labyrinthine organizational structure. In his analysis of the bureaucracy in Kafka's *Schloß*, Axel Dornemann[26] argues that the castle authority is a labyrinth. He uses the term *labyrinthine* metaphorically to describe the bewildering structure of the castle bureaucracy, which negates the autonomy of the individual (106-108). This is a fair assessment of the bureaucracy, but this argument tends to overlook the role (and guilt) of the individual seekers (K. and Josef K.) in Kafka's texts. Bettina Küter describes the hallways with countless doors at the inn in *Das Schloß* as labyrinthine.[27] I would argue that the configurations of the inn mirror those of the court chancellery in *Der Prozeß*. In my view, Küter's understanding of the labyrinthine structure of specific buildings is too narrow. I would argue that these buildings are part of a larger city labyrinth, and this enables the reader to see the court in *Der Prozeß* as part of a larger cultural phenomenon.

3.3 Theseus and the Minotaur: K. and the Court

In a historical context, the theme of the city in *Der Prozeß* signifies the breakdown of cultural codes in Europe of the early twentieth century. Eagleton identifies the dominant cultural codes in bourgeois society in terms of the aesthetic, a discourse which posits an ideal of autonomous individuals capable of freely submitting their own bodily domain (*Natur*) to the laws of the mind (*Geist*). The disharmony between nature and civilization is a symptom of a cultural crisis in the depicted society, suggesting that the individuals do not know how to relate intellectually to the corporal aspect of existence. This in turn corresponds to von der Brück's reading of the Minotaur: the Minotaur, with the head of an animal and the body of a man, represents a mythological representation of humanity's struggle to confront its *Natur*.

Similarly, the court in *Der Prozeß* demands that defendants write an ethical interpretation of life in terms of corporality. Ronell was one of the first critics to point out that the castle administration in *Das Schloß* is a massive interpretative apparatus (221); and the same holds true for the court system in *Der Prozeß*. The court is a massive bureaucracy for the processing of texts (the files of defendants). The lawyer Huld frequently meets with court officials to discuss defendants' files. Huld explains that countless court officials analyze the files before passing them on to superiors. So many officials can examine these texts that court functionaries in the lower echelons often do not know what happens to the files. In some cases, working with the texts takes up nearly every waking hour of members of the court. The washer woman states that the magistrate often works with files well into the night.

In *Der Prozeß*, the court evaluates the defendants' relationship to the body. This can be discerned from the two law books in the apartment building on Julius Street and Block's statements about his trial. Block's case begins just after his wife dies; in other words, after a twofold change in his relationship to the body: the loss of an erotic relationship, and the confrontation with death. Significantly, Block has not found the right intellectual sustenance. Rather, as a grain dealer, he has a commercial, i.e., material relationship to food. His fellow defendant K. sees references to the body on the cover of the two law books. On one, K. sees images of the body: a picture of a naked man and woman sitting next to each other. The other book, entitled "Die Plagen welche Grete von ihrem Manne Hans zu erleiden hatte," may well concern the figures Hänsel and Gretel from Grimm's fairy tale after they have grown into adults. As children, their desire for food nearly led them to their death, but they survived the test in the woods by virtue of their character. The title of the law book implies that after returning to civilization their character was ruined.

For defendants, the trial is the process of finding the law, the needed ethical sustenance. Writing an interpretation of life is a task with religious overtones, given the language of the court. The German terms for the court system can have both legal and religious signification: *Urteil, Gericht, Schuld*, and *Legende*, the term used for a genuine acquittal. The German word *Legende* can mean either a nonhistorical story handed down by tradition or the life history of a saint.[28] In addition, the crowd at the hearing is wearing black uniforms much like the clergy. Finally, K. sees a chancellery in both the cathedral and on Julius Street.

In addition, the court, like the church, makes frequent use of candles. There is a candle on Fräulein Bürstner's night table, in Huld's bedroom, in the storage room of the bank, and, of course, in the cathedral. In Huld's kitchen, Block holds a candle which he extinguishes while he converses with K. Naturally, the candles provide light for reading texts, but this points to the crisis of the cultural tradition in two respects. First, the candles cast only a dim light, a metaphor for the difficulties which interpreters face. Second, the candle represents an old-fashioned, if not obsolete source of light in modern industrial society. This indicates that the court's interpretative methods are likewise inadequate for understanding texts composed in the modern world.

In fact, the world depicted in Kafka's text is one from which God is absent. On a painting in the cathedral, K. is surprised that the image of Christ is missing from a painting of his burial. The power of the court is not based on a transcendent authority, nor are there spiritual moorings for the universal ethical laws which are supposed to govern the body. As a result, the female body becomes a token in abusive power relations among the men of an inscrutible world authority. In *Das Schloß*,[29] for example, the castle authorities routinely summon young women for their own pleasure. In *Der Prozeß*, the magistrate and Bertold the student aggressively pursue the washer woman whose husband lacks the status to prevent their liaisons.

With the absence of a transcendent authority, the court itself cannot apply ethical laws to corporality. The lasciviousness of some court officials is actually a symptom of the cultural crisis. Hence, it is appropriate that the structure of the court is represented as a labyrinth, a signifier of the crisis. The representation of the court is difficult to reconcile with its demand that defendants define the ethical basis of human existence in writing. The defendant must therefore have a more reflective stance towards ontological issues than the court for which they interpret.

Naturally K.'s personality structure has come under close scrutiny. Some critics, such as Heinz Politzer[30] and Gerhard Kaiser,[31] see K. as a typical hardworking individual, while others, such as Sokel (147) and the Marxist Helmut Richter,[32] argue that K. is a typical modern businessman who is engrossed in his career to the exclusion of nearly everything else. On this basis, it is possible to advance the view that K. has hidden his true self, and his guilt is therefore existential (Emrich 269, Politzer 173). I would argue that K.'s guilt is symptomatic of the collapse of idealist aesthetics: his guilt stems from his inability to subject the realm of the body to ethical laws, and this manifests itself in the tension between sensuality and ethics even before the trial begins. The nature of K.'s social contacts reveals profound tension between sensuality and ethics. Once a week, he visits the bar girl Elsa for sexual pleasure. But apparently, bodily gratification does not fulfill a deeper need to find meaning in life. Not surprisingly then, K. frequently eats and drinks in a tavern with acquaintances, most of whom are lawyers and judges. His one friend is district attorney Hasterer. K.'s affinity for legal affairs has not gone unnoticed by business clients. The industrialist likens K.'s perspicacious reading of business texts to that of a lawyer. "K. ist fast ein Advokat" (Kafka, *Der Prozeß* 164). This implies that K.'s hermeneutical methods are essentially the same as those of the court officials who operate with legal discourse. In short, K. can be seen as a lascivious official who applies legal reading strategies to texts. If K. is to move through the labyrinth, he will have to develop a more reflective orientation in life.

3.4 House

The actual starting point of K.'s movement in the labyrinth is frequently his house, in which he is arrested. In the Western literary tradition, the motif of the house provides information on figures' attitudes towards life (Daemmrich 165). In *Der Prozeß*, the contrasting spatial patterns of K.'s house are actually based on the constituent elements of the labyrinth. The one side is the space of light, food, and community, whereas K.'s room is the space of darkness, hunger, and isolation. The motifs of light and darkness appear in conjunction with the motifs of food and love, which, as noted earlier, give the reader insight into the figures' attitudes towards corporality. The connection of these motif and thematic patterns in the house indicates that the figures' relationships to the body determine the kind of involvement they have with others.

To be sure, with the exception of Fräulein Bürstner and Fräulein Montag, K.'s neighbors do not actually appear in the text. K. could not possibly discover this because he is not interested in his neighbors in the least. Information about his fellow tenants is presented the one time K. goes over to the other side of the house. Ironically, he speaks with Fräulein Montag, who tries to discourage him from contacting another neighbor, Fräulein Bürstner.

K. converses with Fräulein Montag in the dining room, which has a window looking out to a house in the distance. During their dialogue, the sun shines on the house. Significantly, this is the only time in the text that sunlight appears. This event establishes the motif cluster of light-house: by motif cluster, I mean the fusion of two or more distinct motifs into a single, recurring configuration. In this case, the motif cluster indicates that the figures have an attitude towards life, as signified by the motif of the house, that enables them to gain understanding. Further details in the dining room illustrate the way in which individuals can grow intellectually.

The dining room is set up for the weekly Sunday dinner. The motif of food is a clear sign that K.'s neighbors receive sustenance. The fact that the dinner is on Sunday reveals further that these weekly gatherings are far more than an opportunity for the tenants to still their hunger pangs at the same time. Rather, the Sunday dinner is a metaphor for the ethical sustenance which can be found on the other side of K.'s house. By contrast, K. eats alone on the other side before his conversation with Fräulein Montag.

Naturally, it is impossible to draw definitive conclusions about the neighbors' attitudes towards life since the tenants are nowhere to be seen in the text. Still, the motifs of light and food suggest two possible interpretations. Conceivably, K.'s neighbors already understand life and have found the intellectual sustenance needed to form a kind of community. Alternatively, it is possible that K. can find the meaning of life by engaging them. Along these lines, the other occurrences of the motifs of light and food appear in conjunction with figures capable of human love, the commitment to help others (Daemmrich 215-216). On Julius Street, a number of tenants try to help K. find his way, even though many are busy preparing food for sick or frail tenants. K.'s uncle worries that K. is not getting the proper sustenance, saying "Du bist ein wenig abgemagert" (Kafka, *Der Prozeß* 118). The uncle then arranges a meeting with the attorney Huld.

In either event, there can be no doubt that K. should move towards the other tenants. In terms of the labyrinth, that would amount to taking the path to the light. K., however, spends most of his time on the other side of the house, where his bedroom is located. It is clearly the wrong side because after his arrest, his bedroom is frequently described as being dark. Without the right food, K. is ignorant of the ethical law to apply to his bodily domain. He still must sense the need to find the meaning of life, for his trial begins when he reponds to a somatic lack, hunger. Dazed and half awake, K. rings the bell for breakfast. Both his hunger and mental state signal his confusion about bodily incompleteness. To K.'s astonishment, not food but a "Gericht" of a much different kind appears at his door to arrest him.

K. must now begin the process of interpreting life. Eventually, K. will have to present his understanding of life in a text, but at this early stage, K. cannot be expected to know that. After all, the guards never explain the nature of the court to him, and K. asserts that he has never heard of the court. Paradoxically, he appears to accept the logic of the court even though he claims to know nothing about the court. Without any prompting, he presents two documents (texts): his bicycle license and, more importantly, his birth certificate, a document that attests to his physical presence in the world. The guards' derisive laughter reveals the futility of K.'s actions. It is not enough to certify the fact that he was born into the world as an empirical being. Rather, he must give meaning to his life from birth to death.

By accepting their order to return to his room, he accepts the constraints of the court's discourse. This is the same mistake that the man from the country makes in the parable. The man from the country would have to break through the court's restraints to move toward the light. In K.'s case, the path to the light leads to his neighbors. To be sure, K. has the opportunity to go to the other side of the house where his neighbors have apparently found sustenance. An antechamber separates the two sides of the house. Both K.'s bedroom and the adjoining living room have doors which open to the antechamber. The doors in both rooms are first presented when K. considers entering the antechamber. Both times the doors are unguarded, but K. is afraid of provoking the court. As a quester, however, K. makes a serious mistake: he fails to move to the light.

Hence, K. chooses not to go to the other side where he could find the ethical basis for living. To do so, he would have to engage intellectually the source of corporal incompleteness, death. But K. shows no willingness to confront his mortality. On the command of the guards, he retreats into his bedroom, and contemplates suicide as a way of foiling his captors. K. then quickly dismisses any thought of suicide, decrying it as "senseless." Death is anything but senseless. It is the very precondition of making sense of life.

The darkness in K.'s room on the night of the arrest signifies his intellectual confusion. Subsequently, there is no mention of light in his room. I would argue that his intellectual disorientation is a product of his material relationship to the body. Since he has not discovered the law, he cannot control his bodily drives. Indeed, the night of the arrest, he foregoes dinner and makes lascivious advances towards Fräulein Bürstner. K. comes to her to apologize for the unauthorized use of her room; the inspector formally arrests K. in her room. K. even reenacts the arrest to illustrate the events of the morning. K.'s meeting with Fräulein Bürstner could yield him important benefits if he can engage in a meaningful exchange with her. She expresses the willingness to help him and her keen interest in legal affairs.

But K. is overpowered by his physical attraction to her. Instead of seeking her advice, he tries to trap her in a corner of the room, where he kisses her "wie ein durstiges Tier" (Kafka, *Der Prozeß* 42). By acting on his sensuous impulses, K is reduced to a thirsty (variation of hunger) animal in nature. The motif of darkness recurs in scenes in which K. is again captive to his libidinal drives. Further, the occurrence of darkness expands the motif and thematic patterns which illustrate K.'s material relationship to corporality. Since K. remains in the darkness of his house, he must move through the city-labyrinth in search of the path to the light.

3.5 Search: K.'s Pattern of Movements in the City

K. makes a series of movements in order to address his trial. It seems that K. is continually leaving his apartment or his office to meet with court officials or individuals who, he hopes, will give him useful advice. Each meeting takes place in the city or, in other words, in the enclosed space of the city. K., to be sure, has the chance to leave the city since the court has granted him freedom of motion. But K. actually chooses to stay in the city-labyrinth. The chapter "Fahrt zur Mutter," in which K. travels to a nearby town to visit his mother, was removed from the novel. During the trial, K.'s uncle invites him to his house in the country, but K. declines, claiming that going to the country would be "Schuldbewußtsein" (Kafka, *Der Prozeß* 119).

Within the confines of the city, K. confers on his trial in a variety of places. The settings include K.'s apartment, his bank office, the cathedral, Huld's apartment, the court hall, the apartments on the Juliustraße, the chancellery, and Titorelli's apartment. The list of the settings shows a variety of different places where the plot unfolds. However, there is considerable mirroring of a relatively small number of spaces. Essentially, the layout of K.'s apartment serves as a template for most of the other layouts. The first chapter begins in K.'s bedroom, the living room, and Fräulein Bürstner's room. Each of the three adjoining rooms has a window which looks out across the street to another building. In addition, each room has a door to a common antechamber. There is a second door in K.'s room which opens to the living room. The living room, in turn, has a third door which opens to Fräulein Bürstner's room.

On the other side of the antechamber, there is a hallway to the kitchen: near the hallway is the dining room where K. speaks with Fräulein Montag. The dining room has a window which looks out to a house. The floorplan of the apartment is mirrored in two other settings: K.'s office at the bank and Huld's apartment. The former has essentially the same layout as the side of K.'s apartment where the arrest takes place: there is a door to an antechamber and another to the next office, that of the assistant manager. The layout of the other side of K.'s apartment closely resembles that of Huld's apartment. Both have an antechamber and a hallway leading to the kitchen. The counterpart to the dining room in K.'s apartment is Huld's office with its three large windows.

Additional settings mirror one another as well. For instance, the chancellery also corresponds to the floor of the bank where K.'s office is located. In both locations, there is a long hallway with numerous doors to offices. Inside the offices, officials work at tables, pouring over texts (court documents). Clearly, the chancellery in the attic of Titorelli's apartment building is a repetition of the chancellery on Juliusstraße. Since these two layouts appear to mirror that of the bank, we can consider all three as expansions of the basic layout of K.'s apartment.

The chancellery also shares a number of features with the cathedral. There are benches on either side of the main path, the hallway of the chancellery, and the aisle of the cathedral. Moreover, he comes across individuals in both places who could give him information to help interpret his case. In the chancellery K. speaks with three employees of the court: the servant, the woman, and the information officer. In the cathedral there are a servant, an old woman, and the chaplain who explains the parable to K.

While K. appears to move to a large number of different places, in reality he takes the same path in space. As a result, K. is moving for the most part to different sections of the same two spaces in his apartment and the chancellery. Even though K. goes to unfamiliar places, he is in effect moving in a circle. There is only an illusion of progress since he effectively traverses the same path. In sections 3.7 and 3.8, I wish to point out the connection between K.'s relationship to the body and his lack of progress in his search for the meaning of life.

3.6 Path-Door-Darkness

The quester must explore a series of paths in the labyrinth in order to find the one that leads out to the light. K. moves through the city-labyrinth for his trial, the search for the meaning of life. When he goes to address his trial, he has a choice of paths marked by doors. K. actually chooses the path to darkness on three occasions: his hearing on Julius Street, his return to Julius Street, and his first visit with Huld. This represents a recurrence of the pattern from his arrest: K. ends up in dark spaces which, as I showed earlier in section 3.6, for the most part mirror his apartment. In the analysis of the house, I argued that the darkness signifies K.'s material relationship to the body. In the three movements on which I will now concentrate, I will focus on the recurrence of the motif of darkness and its variations, the motifs of fog or haze, to draw a full picture of K.'s relationship to corporality.

K.'s first movement comes only a week after his arrest, when he is summoned to a hearing. K. has difficulties finding the hearing room because it could potentially be in any of the countless apartments in the building on Julius Street. In his frustration, K. is ready to give up when he knocks at a door on the fifth floor. Significantly, the washer woman, who is the object of desire for several members of the court, pulls him into the hearing room. That she leads him into a hazy room reinforces the connection between darkness (haze) and eros. K.'s subsequent actions expand the configurations associated with eros.

K. must go before the magistrate who awaits him behind a desk. The scene basically mirrors the setting in Fräulein Bürstner's room during the arrest: a member of the court sits behind a desk with papers, in this case the magistrate's notebook. The notebook is a clear indication that the verbal exchange in the hearing is being conducted in order to compose a written text. In fact, the following week the washer woman tells K. that the magistrate spent hours preparing a text based on the hearing. K., however, treats the dialogue in the hearing as a power struggle. He seizes the notebook from the magistrate, and, as if to demonstrate his contempt for the very idea of writing for the court, cavalierly drops the notebook on the table. In his statements, K. also tries to dominate the communicative process. He launches an attack against the court, first dismissing the trial as "nichts," then ridiculing the guards from his arrest as juvenile pranksters. The reference to the guards sheds light on K.'s narrative strategy, if such a diatribe can be termed a strategy. K. is simply recounting the events from his arrest and buttresses his tirade with assumptions about corruption in the court. While K. may be correct with some of his charges, his unreflective stance is a sign of intellectual confinement.

K.'s harsh words stem from underlying aggression. He surprises himself by making pointed utterances in his first statement: "Was er gesagt hatte, war scharf, schärfer als er es beabsichtigt hatte, aber doch richtig" (Kafka, *Der Prozeß* 55). K.'s aggressive gestures mark the definitive breakdown of the hearing. He strikes the table with his fist. In the end, his violent impulse reaches the point where he is ready to punch the members of the court who block his way to the exit.

K.'s aggression makes any substantive dialogue at the hearing impossible. The individual must have meaningful exchanges with a wide spectrum of people to understand being. By contrast, K.'s actions towards the magistrate seemed designed to prevent an exchange. This is not the only time that K. displays aggressive behavior towards others. He treats Frau Grubach abusively after discussing the arrest with her and later inflicts pain on the hapless Block. Both figures are fully prepared to help K., and Block even relates to K. his experiences in writing petitions. In each case, K. brings a dialogue which could potentially give him important insights to an abrupt end. There is little likelihood that K. can transcend his own horizons or the discourse of the court if he does not engage the views of others. Thus, his intellectual disorientation, as signified by the haze in the room, is caused in no small part by his aggression.

At the beginning of the discussion of the hearing, I mentioned that the haze is linked to eros, a symptom of K.'s material relationship to the body. Eros and aggression are closely connected in that they are both symptoms of the same phenomenon. The connection is underscored by the simultaneity of aggressive and erotic outbursts near the end of the hearing. Just as K.'s diatribe reaches its climax, Bertold the student grabs the washer woman and embraces her in the corner of the room. Bertold's actions must be seen as a reflection of K.'s own sensuous drives. The scene in the corner of the room mirrors K.'s embracing and kissing of Fräulein Bürstner in the corner of her bedroom; further, both assaults occur after K. recounts the events of the arrest. The scene at the hearing also foreshadows K.'s advances towards the washer woman the following week. The link between eros and aggression in *Der Prozeß* corresponds to Lacan's[33] findings on aggression. Lacan traces aggression back the libidinal drives. He observes that patients with aggressive tendencies sometimes struggle to make linguistic utterances (19). While K. has no difficulty speaking at the hearing, his distorted account of the arrest lacks meaningful content. In short, K.'s aggression represents a varied form of his desire for the female body. Thus, the haze in the room indicates that K.'s intellectual confinement is worsened by his failure to exchange meaning, a failure which is ultimately rooted in his material relationship to corporality.

The nexus of darkness, eros, and aggression recurs on K.'s return visit to the building on Julius Street. K. proceeds directly to the room of his hearing. This time, the room is not explicitly described as hazy, although the chancellery upstairs is. The only person in the room when K. first arrives is the washer woman. She expresses the hope that K. will bring about some improvements in her vulnerable position in the court. K. sees her desire for change as the basis for exchanging favors. "Wenn ich aber dabei auch Ihnen irgendwie nützlich sein kann, werde ich es natürlich sehr gerne tun. Nicht etwa nur aus Nächstenliebe, sondern außerdem deshalb, weil auch Sie mir helfen können" (Kafka, *Der Prozeß* 66). K. asks that she show him the law books. He may actually have the right idea. If he can understand the court's legal codes, he may be better able to develop his own interpretation of life, thereby providing the culture with a new model of human relations. But K. never reads the texts, only the covers which he condemns as obscene.

K.'s view of the court changes his attitude towards the washerwoman. He doubts that she can help him since, he assumes, she only has contact with the lustful delinquents in the lower echelons of the court. Implicitly, K. rejects the idea of exchanging help with an inferior partner. But as he becomes aware of her apparent attraction for him, he begins to think of her body as a useful object or token in his power struggle against the court:

> Es könnte sich dann einmal der Fall ereignen, daß der Untersuchungsrichter nach mühevoller Arbeit an Lügenberichten über K. in später Nacht das Bett der Frau leer fand. Und leer deshalb, weil sie K. gehörte, weil...dieser üppige, gelenkige, warme Körper...durchaus nur K. gehörte. (Kafka, *Der Prozeß* 72-73)

Two aspects of this quote deserve special attention. First, K. shows no indication of liking the washerwoman as a person. Gaining her favor serves a larger goal, namely, getting back at the magistrate. Second, K.'s line of thinking makes a connection between texts ("Lügenberichte") and the body. At the hearing, K. takes a text (the notebook) away from the magistrate. Now, K. quite literally contemplates taking away a body ("dieser üppige, gelenkige, warme Körper") from the magistrate. Hence, for K., the female body displaces the text in the struggle against the court. As a result, K. effectively reverses the process by which the defendant must produce a written interpretation: the desire for the body must be transformed into the desire for understanding.

Bertold's sudden appearance interferes with K.'s calculations. In a repetition of the incident during the hearing, Bertold carries off the washer woman. The connection between eros and aggression is reinforced by the fact that Bertold and K., who are both attracted to the washer woman, make threatening gestures and statements to each other. Further, K. tries to trip the fleeing Bertold while the latter actually snaps at K. like a stray animal. This underscores the animal-like nature of uncontrolled sexuality in the text, a configuration that first occurs when K. kisses Fräulein Bürstner like a "thirsty animal."

K. sees Bertold's seizure of the washer woman as his first defeat at the hands of the court. But K. assures himself that he can eventually turn the tables on Bertold because he possesses a female body (that of Elsa) with more value than that of the washer woman:

> Und er stellte sich die allerlächerlichste Szene vor, die es zum Beispiel geben würde, wenn dieser klägliche Student, dieses aufgeblasene Kind, dieser krumme Bartträger vor Elsas Bett knien und mit gefalteten Händen um Gnade bitten würde. (Kafka, *Der Prozeß* 75)

At this point, K. has gone one step further than merely substituting a woman's body for a text. He effectively substitutes one female body for another, as if they were tokens. There can be no question that K. is abjectly failing in his attempt to find an ethical basis of life. The haze (darkness) which signifies his intellectual confusion indicates that he has still not found the right path in the labyrinth.

In his first meeting with Huld, K. actually has the option of moving to the light or the darkness. A reluctant K. is compelled by his insistent uncle to consult with the attorney Huld, a friend of K.'s uncle. K.'s hesitation is a further sign of his contradictory attitude towards the trial, but his uncle demands that he take immediate action in his case. The uncle is so determined to make progress in K.'s case that he lets no barrier stand in his way to Huld. Indeed, the uncle forces his way into Huld's bedroom, in spite of the protestations of the maid Leni that Huld is ill.

Although the figure of the uncle appears in only one chapter of *Der Prozeß*, his function in the text must be given careful scrutiny; for the uncle represents a contrast figure to the man in the parable "Vor dem Gesetz." The man from the country fails to find the right food since he remains insatiable (*unersättlich*) to the end. The uncle, who also comes from the country, notices that K. is not getting the right nourishment. He offers to take care of K., presumably by feeding him, so that K. will be strong enough for the challenges ahead. The man from the country stops at the first of a series of doors and waits to be granted permission to enter. The uncle displays none of his counterpart's passivity. He rings until the front door is opened, bursts through the door to the apartment, and finally enters through Huld's bedroom door. Whereas the man from the country never reaches the law, the uncle makes his way to Huld, who happens to be meeting with a representative of the law, the director of the chancellery. Finally, the man from the country does not see the light during most of his futile conversations with the guard. The uncle, however, finds the light (he takes a candle from the night table) at the *beginning* of his exchange with Huld. The uncle's movement is even more significant since Huld's apartment mirrors the side of K.'s apartment, which includes the dining room which is exposed to sunlight. This is, of course, the place where K.'s neighbors share meals together.

In light of the recurrence of this spatial configuration, it is clear that K. has a real opportunity to find the needed intellectual food, the law. K. can count on the help of his uncle, a resolute, tireless man from the country who already has the light. Additionally, he could exchange views with a powerful court official who is polite and forthcoming to his uncle, and an experienced defense lawyer who takes a keen interest in his case. In fact, it is quite likely that Huld and the director of the chancellery are discussing K.'s case when he arrives. That would certainly explain why Huld is already quite familiar with the case, and why the director waits for hours after K. disappears into Huld's office.

K. shows no interest in an intellectual exchange, but as I shall point out in a moment, in an exchange of a much different kind. He quickly becomes bored with the dialogue between his uncle and Huld. K. is only too pleased to leave the room to find the cause of a disturbing noise, and is even happier when Leni leads him into Huld's office across the hall. But this is a movement from the light to the darkness; K. has trouble seeing at first. Leni offers K. help on the condition that he become her lover. K. is initially hesitant because he already has a lover, Elsa. Earlier, K. compares the value of the washer woman to that of Elsa. He now measures the usefulness of Leni in terms of Elsa. By relenting to Leni, K. exchanges Elsa for her. Leni even describes K.'s decision as an exchange: '"Sie haben mich eingetauscht!' rief sie von Zeit zu Zeit 'sehen Sie, nun haben Sie mich eingetauscht!'" (Kafka, *Der Prozeß* 135). Since K. sets up an exchange system of women, the female body is, in effect, a commodity for him. By extension, K.'s heretofore empty dialogues can be seen as a reified system of verbal exchange. Indeed, this conclusion is supported by K.'s likening his trial to a business transaction while writing the petition.

Thus, the growing darkness, the progression from the haze to the darkness of the night, is a sign that K., because of his material orientation in life, is increasingly unable to reflect on the meaning of life. As a result, he is essentially retracing the same path to darkness in the labyrinth. Ironically, the path to the light is not far away in spatial terms. His neighbors gather on the other side of the antechamber and at Huld's; his uncle sits just across the hallway.

3.7 Path-Door-Dead End

Clearly, one reason for K.'s lack of success on his quest is that he turns down the path to darkness. In the configurations of K.'s house, the motif of darkness initially appears in conjunction with eros, a cipher for K.'s material relationship to the body. As he repeatedly appears in dark spaces, the manifestations of his material way of being grow to encompass aggression and his reified system of exchange. I would now like to explore an additional aspect of K.'s relationship to corporality, his fear of death. This fear of death leaves him helpless in a dead end of the labyrinth. In the final analysis, K's fear of death is a symptom of his reified way of being.

I am referring to the scene in the chancellery on Julius Street. The significance of this episode can be best understood by comparing K.'s walk through the chancellery with his movement through the lower four floors of the same building. Both movements are important stages of his search in the labyrinth. There is a main path, a hallway, which is intersected by other paths marked by doors. To find his way in the labyrinth, the quester must explore a variety of paths; this would necessitate opening the doors and interacting with the people on the other side. When K. appears on the lower four floors, he moves down the hallway, the main path, in his search for the site of his hearing. K. does not really explore the intersecting paths marked by doors. He notes that most of the doors are open, allowing him to look into the apartments. K. observes numerous women preparing food, while others are lying in bed. The occurrence of food invites a metaphorical reading of this scene. Moreover, it is Sunday, the day on which K.'s fellow tenants eat together. The need for ethical sustenance is revealed by the sickness, or bodily suffering, of the tenants of the apartment building on Julius Street. The sickness underscores the suffering which the lower classes endure in modern society. The sickness afflicting their bodies can be seen as a cipher for the oppressive socio-economic factors which leave the tenants in squalor. Near the gate of the building, K. discovers storage docks for commercial goods ("Warenmagazine"). The docks belong to the firms whose names stand on the wall. K. recognizes some of the firms from his dealings at the bank. The reference to commodities suggests that the bodies of members of the lower class have become reified in modern society. According to Klotz, the reification of the body is a feature of the theme of the city (153). K. treats the female body as a commodity, and is involved in the process of reification through his work at the bank.

On a broader level, K., as a successful businessman, personifies an intellectual tendency, instrumental reason, which causes the reification of the body. Reification tears fissures in aesthetic discourse as Eagleton defines it. Reification is caused by the external imposition of the laws of (instrumental) reason on the body. Whereas reason in the Enlightenment is supposed to promote the general good, instrumental reason is seen as a means of advancing the bourgeoisie's rise to power. Instrumental reason amounts to a tool for calculating a way of achieving the materialistic goals of the middle class. I would argue that the conflict between nature, the realm of the body, and instrumental reason occurs when workers sell their labor on the labor market. Individuals sell their labor at a price determined by the rational expectations of the buyer and seller. For workers, labor can be understood as a function of the body's ability to perform work. Georg Lukács[34] maintains that labor is sold as a commodity, or as a thing with material qualities. By extension, the source of the workers labor power, their bodies, becomes reified as well. The bodies of workers are therefore subjected to external laws of reason, the rational calculation of the owners.

If sickness is a metaphor for reification, then it is understandable why so many residents of the apartment building help K. Should he find a new intellectual law to govern the realm of the body, his insight could serve as a basis for more humane social relations. K., however, does not show any interest in them, for he does not cross through the doorway to talk with them. Further, he intentionally has empty exchanges with them: he pretends to be looking for "Tischler Lanz" in order to disguise the fact that he is looking for the place of the hearing. Thus, the fact that he does not move down the paths indicated by the doors reveals his unwillingness to engage the tenants.

K. is easily able to traverse four floors since he has only superficial contact with them. Yet the following week, he collapses before making his way through the chancellery located in the top floor of the same building. It is highly unlikely that the walk through the chancellery tires him since the chancellery has essentially the same layout as the lower floors. In the chancellery, there are intersecting hallways with numerous wooden doors on either side. The doors lead to offices in which, in all likelihood, court officials are busy working. This would explain why defendants wait anxiously outside in the hallway and why the court servant who escorts K. comes upstairs to deliver a message. The spatial configurations of the chancellery are also quite similar to those of the "Herrenhof" inn in *Das Schloß* in which Landvermesser K. meets with Bürgel. Afterwards, texts are distributed from door to door to the castle bureaucrats. In light of this, there can be little doubt that the court officials in *Der Prozeß* are going over texts in their offices.

I chose to cover the probable scene behind the doors of the chancellery to point out the most significant difference between the hallways on the lower floors and the one in the chancellery. The real difference is not the spatial configurations of the hallways, for they are virtually identical, but the people in the hallways. Effectively, the tenants are replaced by court officials. If K. is to have intellectual exchanges, he would have to have a series of discussions with powerful court authorities, not with destitute families. The court, however, has removed itself behind closed doors. That would apparently negate the very possibility of a dialogue with the court. Nonetheless, the success of K.'s uncle in reaching both Huld and, significantly, the director of the chancellery, shows that resolute individuals can force their way through doors to meet with court officials. In the chancellery, having discussions with members of the court entails going from office to office. K. must explore the paths of the labyrinth marked by the office doors by having communicative exchanges with court officials. The prospect of having exchanges certainly has something to do with K.'s collapse. The air in the chancellery is especially stifling because of the heavy "Parteienverkehr," exchanges between court and defendants. As the configurations in "Vor dem Gesetz" indicate, reflecting on death is the precondition of understanding communicative exchanges.

Given the similarity of the configurations of the chancellery with those of "Vor dem Gesetz," I would argue that as K. walks down the hallway, he is approaching the crucial encounter with death. Like the man from the country, K. stops in front of a series of doors. K. then stands opposite two representatives of the court in a doorway: the woman and the information officer. Suddenly, K. becomes an old man. Weakened and exhausted, K. collapses; not only is K. physically debilitated, he also has difficulty talking. Even as an old man, the man from the country is able to overcome his physical weakness when he sees the light, the insight that stems from acknowledging death. At this point, the frailty of his body allows him to pose only one question. K. does not see light but is instead covered by black soot (motif of darkness). Consequently, whereas the man from the country finally has one exchange with the guard, K.'s communicative ability breaks down completely. He even has trouble hearing what the information officer and the woman say to him.

The one significant difference between the configurations in the chancellery and in the parable, the displacement of the motif of light by the motif of darkness, must provide information on a corresponding difference in K.'s actions. Unlike the man from the country, K. does not gain any awareness of death. Further, the motif of darkness signifies K.'s material relationship to the body, which is manifested by eros and aggression. That pattern is now expanded by K.'s fear of death.

The mind-body aspect of K.'s existential dread points to a broader cultural context than has been discussed in previous analyses of K.'s dread. Critics, for the most part existentialist critics, have attributed K.'s dread to conflicts in the figure. In this, critics follow Sokel, who argues that K. experiences the conflict between his "pure" and "social self" (140). Josef Mense[35] and Jürg Beat Honegger[36] maintain that K. is plagued by his desire for human love but his inability to give or receive it. But more crucially, the fear of death is, in a historical context, a manifestation of the tension between nature and spirit, a tension which can in part be caused by reification. Thomas Anz[37] maintains that the fear of death is one manifestation of existential dread ("Angst"). According to Anz, the first symptoms of dread in Western civilization became visible in the 18th century, in the midst of the Enlightenment. Significantly, this was the time when the foundation of idealist aesthetics was being laid: at this time, philosophers were developing theories of an autonomous subject whose individual development hinges on its own powers of reflection and self-regulation. Freed from the shackles of external authorities, individuals must now rely on their own faculties to develop their identities. In "Historizität der Angst,"[38] Anz argues that dread can be triggered by the inherent difficulties in forming an identity. Dieter Claessens[39] maintains that dread can also give rise to aggression, a pattern which is certainly consistent with K.'s actions. In Kafka's works, dread is experienced by individuals who endure the conflict between the mind and sensuality.[40] The tension between sensuality and the intellect potentially undermines the Enlightenment notion of the autonomous subject capable of imposing the laws of reason on its own somatic domain.

K.'s dread prevents him from having the pivotal experience in the labyrinth, the encounter with death. In a sense, he has created his own dead end. Concomitant with the manifestation of K.'s fear of death is the revelation of a new aspect of K.'s reified way of being. To find the meaning of life, the ethical law, he must contemplate death with the ultimate aim of taking a reflective stance towards corporality. Such a shift in K.'s way of being is the outcome of the transformation ("Verwandlung") which K. believes the onlooking woman and information officer expect from him. After all, "Verwandlung" is the term used to denote Gregor Samsa's bodily transformation. But since he does not confront death, K. actually reinforces his material relationship to corporality. "K. sagte nichts, sah nicht einmal auf, er duldete es, daß die zwei über ihn wie über eine Sache verhandelten, es war ihm sogar am liebsten" (Kafka, *Der Prozeß* 89). K. lets them talk about him as a "Sache", as if he were an thing. By designating himself as an object, K. implicitly suggests that his own body is reified. This represents a regression to a material state, especially since his mind, "Geist", is completely helpless.

The motif of darkness (soot) signifies K.'s near complete disorientation. He has blundered down a dark dead end in the labyrinth and cannot find his way out. Indeed, K. must be carried to the exit by the two members of the court. The darkness indicates that K. cannot intellectually engage the views of others because of his attitude towards the body, an attitude which manifests itself through eros, aggression, and the fear of death. It is K.'s fear of death which will lead him to seek intermediaries to handle his case.

3.8 Window-Fog

At this juncture, K. shows no sign of finding the way out of the labyrinth. In his search, he continually moves back and forth on the same path and runs into a dead end in the chancellery. Further, K.'s range of movement remains limited to dark spaces. The darkness signifies K.'s intellectual confinement, which is a product of his material orientation in life. K.'s way of being precludes reflection on his own mortality, a failure which could potentially undermine his quest to find the meaning of life. Because he has not found the meaning of life on his own, K. now moves through the labyrinth to seek helpers (Huld and Titorelli) who might guide his quest for him. The motif patterns at Huld's and Titorelli's indicates the degree to which K. understands their advice on interpreting life.

In both locations, the motif cluster of window-darkness occurs. In his studio, Titorelli has a small window which offers a perspective of fog and smoke. There is no doubt that the view from Huld's window is limited by darkness since K. visits the attorney at night. The motif of the window, as shown in section 3.5, furnishes information on K.'s desire to change his relationship to the world through writing. The motif cluster of window-darkness signifies K.'s confusion about developing a new relationship to others through writing. Indeed, Huld and Titorelli explain possible defenses for K. as writing strategies. To prepare a written text for K., Huld or Titorelli would have to engage in the communicative exchanges at which K. fails so miserably.

Initially, K. hopes that Huld will quickly submit a petition. The lawyer however seems content to wait for the right moment, and elaborates on the difficulties facing defense attornies. The court usually withholds the defendants' files (texts) from the defense. Lawyers often have to guess at the court's evaluation of the defendants by interviewing their clients after hearings. Some attorneys go so far as to steal files. By contrast, Huld relies on his close relationship with court officials. In fact, he dismisses the desperate actions of other lawyers since "honest, personal relations" with the court are the only thing of significance. Huld is using these relations to build an interpretative community of court officials favorably disposed towards K. Huld could then influence the course of K.'s case by exchanging views with the interpreters on K.'s text (the petition).

The one problem with Huld's petition is that it is composed in the court's legal discourse. If Block's petition is a reliable guide, petitions are generally filled with confusing legal formulations that have little to do with the defendant. Worse yet, the petitions are written so as to pass through the labyrinthine court bureaucracy; it is for this reason that Block's petition is replete with flattering references to specific judges. Hence, the texts composed in legal discourse by helpers are marked by the cultural crisis, the loss of intellectual orientation which is siginified by the city-labyrinth.

Lawyers and, by extension, other helpers cannot interpret the defendants' lives for them. Indeed, it appears that K. turns to helpers to relieve himself of the burden of finding the ethical sustenance of life on his own. The defendant is spared the frightening confrontation with death, but for this very reason, defendants cannot find the meaning of their own lives. Hence, it is little wonder that defendants are not the subjects of texts which are supposed to interpret their lives.

Since K. is becoming alarmed with Huld's apparent inactivity, he welcomes the chance to meet with Titorelli, a painter with connections to powerful judges. K.'s hopes are quickly dashed. Before, he had a simple choice: either writing his own petition or letting Huld draft it. Now, Titorelli presents him with three defense strategies: the genuine acquittal, the ostensible acquittal, and the procrastination. Only the innocence of the defendant can bring about the genuine acquittal, according to Titorelli. These rare cases are called "Legenden," which is the term for the biography of a saint. This kind of writing was practiced at a much earlier stage of cultural development. In the modern world, few individuals can show how to improve the world like the early saints. Most defendants opt for the other two defenses which both involve having an intermediary gather information to present as text to the court. To achieve an ostensible acquittal for K., Titorelli would have to write a testimonial on K.'s innocence to important judges. In this case, K. does not write his own interpretation of life, rather Titorelli prepares a standard text handed down from his father. Titorelli would then present the text to important judges. This corresponds to K.'s movement in the chancellery; only now, Titorelli, not K., would conduct a series of exchanges with the court. In all likelihood, K. would have to go to the judges himself. Should enough judges sign the testimonial, he could be set free. However, another judge could reopen the case at any time, thereby forcing K. to repeat the process, starting with a the preparation of a new testimonial.

This never ending sequence reveals that traditional ways of understanding being are no longer adequate. The testimony is an interpretation of life based on the court's discourse. After all, Titorelli, who helps prepare the testimony, is a member of the court. Since the testimony is a standardized text, the same interpretative categories are used to evaluate the life of each individual for whom the testimony is presented. Thus, in the testimony the same (universal) conceptions of being are applied to each individual (defendant). Universal definitions in legal discourse can no longer fully explain the meaning of an individual life, for the defendant or Titorelli must continually present new texts.

For either defense, the defendant cannot produce a definitive understanding of life. The one advantage of the two defenses is that the helper can manipulate legal language so as to prevent a conviction. The court cannot sentence someone who at least seems to make the effort to find the meaning of life. For the procrastination, defendants and their helpers influence the course of the case by staying in close contact with the judge. There is no concerted effort to prepare testimony. The defendant exchanges only inconsequential information in meaningless hearings. The level of information appears to correspond to the importance of the insignificant proceedings.

This essentially describes K.'s experiences at the arrest and hearing, i.e., before he consulted Huld and Titorelli. But in the hearing, K. did not offer so much a defense as an attack on the court. An assistant such as Huld or Titorelli would at least be able to help K. prepare a preliminary defense and win the sympathy of court officials. The motif of darkness reveals that K. does not grasp the significance of the advice which he obtains. If he cannot write a defense of his own, he must find someone who will. K.'s desire to be free of the trial shows that he is neither willing to prepare his own defense, nor give the task to anyone else. His prolonged failure to write is a result of his unwillingness to reflect on himself, a form of intellectual resistance that is rooted in his fear of death. Worse yet, he is unwilling to be the object of reflection: he does not want to be the subject of an interpretative text. Thus, K. eventually fires Huld, the only one who stands between K. and the court.

3.9 Hermeneutical Labyrinth

The motif of darkness is a metaphor for K.'s intellectual confusion, which can ultimately be traced back to K.'s material relationship to the body. This curtails his capability to engage in intellectual exchanges during the initial stages of his movement through the city. When K. does attempt to write his own petition, he approaches the task as if it were a business transaction:

Es gab keine Schuld. Der Prozeß war nichts anderes als ein großes Geschäft, wie er schon oft mit Vorteil für die Bank abgeschlossen hatte, ein Geschäft, innerhalb dessen, wie das die Regel war, verschiedene Gefahren lauerten, die eben abgewehrt werden mußten. Zu diesem Zwecke durfte man allerdings nicht mit Gedanken an

irgendeine Schuld spielen, sondern den Gedanken an den eigenen
Vorteil möglichst festhalten. (Kafka, *Der Prozeß* 153)

This text is not based on intellectual exchanges with others. K.'s way of
writing is clearly shaped by his experience in commercial exchanges in which
he tries to gain an advantage over others. In the end, K. cannot finish his
petition, dismissing it as a senseless task for a senile old man.

It is only logical that K. turns to outside advisors (Huld and Titorelli) who
offer to have exchanges with the court in his place. This is an important step;
if K. cannot write his own ethical interpretation of life, he must let someone
else assume that responsibility for him. But his fear of death renders him
unwilling to engage in self-reflection or to be the object of textual reflection
on the part of his advisors. The increasing darkness in the text is a sign that
K.'s confusion leaves him in great danger of becoming trapped in the city-
labyrinth. K.'s last chance comes when the chaplain summons K. to the
cathedral. The chaplain wants to discuss the trial with K., who he fears, is on
the verge of being found guilty. When asked about the status of his case, K.
assures the chaplain that he is working on his petition and obtaining the help
of women. This is the statement of a deluded man, for K. has shown no
inclination to write and he views women not as helpers but as the prize in his
struggle against the court. In response, the chaplain warns K. that he expects
the wrong kind of help from women and that he deceives himself about the
court. To explain the issue of self-deception (*Täuschung*), the chaplain relates
the parable "Vor dem Gesetz" and identifies the man from the country with
K.

The responses of K. and the chaplain to the parable raise the larger
problem of interpretation. Immediately after hearing the parable, K. asserts
that the guard deceives the man by not informing him that the door is only for
him until it is too late. But the man, the chaplain counters, did not pose the
question before that point. The chaplain then proceeds to recount a variety
of interpretations of the parable. Most focus on the personal qualities of the
guard, his relationship to the law, and his treatment of the man. There is no
consensus since some of the interpretations contradict others. Indeed, there
is no agreement on whether the guard is deceived about the nature of the law.

While K. is talking with only one other individual (the chaplain), he is
effectively having a dialogue with the court's interpreters, who have analyzed
the parable over time. The discussion in the cathedral is similar to K.'s visit
to the chancellery, where he has the opportunity to meet with a series of court
officials. To have exchanges with them, K. would have to test a series of paths

of the labyrinth which are marked by doors. In the cathedral, K. can only have a kind of dialogue with court officials by engaging their interpretations of the parable. Thus, the paths which lead to the court officials are replaced by the interpretations.

Taken together, the interpretations of the parable form a hermeneutical labyrinth. This hermeneutical labyrinth closely resembles Eco's concept of the semiotic labyrinth. Eco applies this term to the notion of the labyrinth among the French encyclopaedists of the 18th century:

> ...the universe of semiosis,...the universe of human culture, must be conceived as structured like a labyrinth...(a) It is structured according to *a network of interpretants*. (b) It is virtually *infinite* because it takes into account multiple interpretations. (Eco 83)

The recurrence of the motif of the labyrinth indicates that the cultural crisis, as signified by the city-labyrinth, has shaped the court's discourse. Like the burrow in "Der Bau," the maze-like structure leaves its creator, the court, in confusion. In the recounting of the interpretations, the man from the country and the guard are linguistic tropes in this complex signifying network. Consequently, the conflicting assumptions and conclusions about the parable show that the signs in the court's discursive network are unstable. This is congruent with the underlying problem of Titorelli's two defenses strategies: the universal (concepts of being) no longer correponds to the individual (life). Thus it is surely not the case that the court or, more specifically, the chaplain deliberately confuses defendants as Sokel argues (202-203). I agree with Nägele, who builds on Emrich's argument that Kafka's works stage the loss of the universal logos, the traditional basis of signification (Nägele 20-21). With respect to *Der Prozeß*, the conflicting interpretations of the parable reflect the absence of a transcendental signifier to anchor meaning (Nägele 28); this state of affairs corresponds to the loss of transcendent authority for the court. Hence, there is no stable center in the court's legal discourse just as there is no center in the city labyrinth.

It would then seem impossible for K. to find his way through the hermeneutical labyrinth. I would argue that the chaplain's willingness to help K. actually offers the latter a glimmer of hope. The chaplain does not defend a particular interpretation. Rather, he explains an array of opinions on the parable. The chaplain therefore represents all the interpreters. If K. can cooperate with him to sort through the views on the parable, K. in effect would work with the interpreters. The one dialogue with the chaplain could make up for K.'s failure to meet with the court officials in the chancellery. Since the chaplain is fully prepared to help him, K. has obtained the cooperation of the interpreters. In "Forschungen eines Hundes," all the dogs must work together to chew through to the marrow in the bone, a metaphor for the meaning of life: "...wären alle Zähne bereit, sie müßten nicht mehr beißen, der Knochen würde sich öffnen und das Mark läge frei dem Zugriff des schwächsten Hündchen" (Kafka, *Beschreibung* 257). It must be emphasized that the willingness to help is the precondition of discovering the food. If the dogs were prepared to chew, it would not even be necessary to bite.

Since the court is characterized by aggressive power relations, it is hardly surprising that court officials have not been able to work together. If K. can work with the chaplain, they would form an interpretative community which would be a model of more meaningful human relations than those of the court. Moreover, if they develop a new understanding of the parable together, it would be a breakthrough for K. and the court. For K., the willingness to sift through the interpretations with the chaplain would correspond to the dogs' willingness to bite into the bone. This is the only means by which he could find his way through the hermeneutical labyrinth.

K., however, becomes disoriented in the hermeneutical labyrinth. He gets lost in the uncertainties and ambiguities of the parable. But K. is used to interpreting business documents on which the value of signs have clear, utilitarian value. He is therefore ill-equipped to examine the interpretations of "Vor dem Gesetz," whose signs have shifting semantic values. K.'s exhaustion signals that he is overwhelmed by the range of alternative views. K.'s pathetic state indicates that he again shies away from self-reflection because the chaplain expressly identifies him with the man from the country in the parable.

By the end of the chaplain's exegesis, the darkness has actually increased because K.'s candle has burned out. Weary and confused, K. is lost in a hermeneutical labyrinth. By extension, he has become trapped in the city-labyrinth as well, for there is not the slightest flicker of light to show him a new path. In the end it is K., not the chaplain, who is no longer prepared to work together to gain understanding. K. now wants to return to the bank and therefore breaks off the discussion with the chaplain. He would much prefer to leave the the bewildering world of interpretation. K. goes back to the realm of a language which reflects the materialistic orientation of society. His confusion is signalled by his exhaustion. He also becomes tired in the chancellery and at Titorelli's: K.'s unwillingness to confront his mortality renders him incapable of transcending his simplistic perspective of the world. By asking for the way out, K. repeats the same sequence of events as in the chancellery: his communicative ability collapses and he has to be taken to the exit.

In the cathedral, K. has essentially reached a guilty verdict on himself. K. neither writes an interpretation of his own, nor does he let his helpers write one for him. In *Der Prozeß*, not finding the law, the ethical basis for life, is tantamount to losing one's way in a hellish, confusing modern world.

3.10 Closing the Circle: the House

In the end, K. is sentenced to death. K. fails to make even a half-hearted attempt to find intellectual sustenance, the ethical law to govern the corporal realm. His executioners come in a scene which mirrors the arrest. Two members of the court appear at his door. Just as K. rings the bell for the guards at his arrest, he actually seems to expect his executioners when they arrive.

The repetition of the arrest illustrates how little K. learns in the one year of the trial. The executioners lead him to a remote quarry at the edge of the city. K. is made to lie on a rock so that his executioners can complete their grisly task. As he awaits his death, K. notices a lone figure in the window of a nearby house:

> Wie ein Licht aufzuckt, so fuhren die Fensterflügel eines Fensters dort auseinander, ein Mensch, schwach und dünn in der Ferne und Höhe, beugte sich mit einem Ruck weit vor und streckte die Arme noch weiter aus. (Kafka, *Der Prozeß* 271-272)

Once again, K. cannot reach the light. The way to the light was just across the antechamber of his house. But he never shows the slightest desire to approach his neighbors. In his search in the city-labyrinth, he consistently takes the path to darkness. Likewise, he never accepts the help that so many individuals (Fräulein Bürstner, the uncle, Huld, and Titorelli) offer him. But no one can help K. as long as he is unwilling to reflect on himself.

The darkness in the quarry signifies K.'s intellectual confinement, his inability to transcend his intellectual horizons in the year of his trial. The motif of darkness, as I have already argued, signifes his material relationship to the body; this attitude towards the body manifests itself in eros, aggression, and the fear of death. Mense argues that death is the only way of attaining freedom for Kafka's figures (81). This implies a kind of deliverance from the fallen world depicted in Kafka's texts (109). But any idea that K. might be attaining freedom is negated by the fact that the executioners hold K. in a vice-like grip as they walk through the city and eventually force him to lie down. K. is sentenced to death because he fails to find the ethical law to govern the body. It is appropriate that K., who is fixated on the *Natur* aspect of being, ends up in a place where nature is dead, a bleak, desolate quarry. The configuration indicates that the individual cannot lead a meaningful existence with a material orientation in life. With such an orientation, the individual becomes lost in a labyrinth, a dark, confusing hell.

3.11 Summary

The motif of the labyrinth in *Der Prozeß* is a signifier of the cultural crisis, the profound intellectual disorientation which undermines value systems that once gave direction to people's lives. The world captured by the city labyrinth is a frightening one in which social relations have become reified. The recurrence of the motif of the labyrinth indicates further that the cultural crisis renders the society incapable of understanding its cultural tradition, a state of affairs represented by the hermeneutical labyrinth. Kafka is, as far as I can tell, the first to use the hermeneutical labyrinth in a *literary* text; this move self-reflexively thematizes the problem of interpretation in modern civilization. It also adds to the enormous burden on defendants who must develop ethical codes (the law) which could regulate the somatic domain. At stake in *Der Prozeß* is the possibility of establishing new ethical and cultural codes through textual (self-) reflection. K.'s movement in the city is an allegory for his progress in learning how to reflect.

The body is not only the object of writing but also the determining factor in his progress in the city labyrinth. The contrasting patterns of light and dark give information about the quester's relationship to corporality. The motif of darkness signifies K.'s intellectual disorientation. K.'s confusion is a result of his material relationship to the body, which in turn is supported by the motifs of dread, eros, and aggression. K.'s response to human embodiment typifies his reified way of being. The only way for individuals to understand being, and thus see the light, is to contemplate death. In mythology the encounter with death is the central event in the quester's movement through the labyrinth. Conceivably, individuals can then develop the ethical codes which will enable them to form meaningful relations to others. The configurations in *Der Prozeß* indicate that developing new cultural codes could open the way for new societal relations to replace the existing reified ones. The analysis of the patterns in the text shows further that the inability to govern the somatic domain leads to abusive, degrading relations among fearful individuals and arbitrary, authoritarian institutional practices. The latter pattern certainly applies to K., who loses his way in the darkness of the labyrinth, failing to write an ethical interpretation of life. *Der Prozeß* presents the reader with a grim world in which the older cultural codes have collapsed and modern individuals do not know how to establish new ones.

CHAPTER 4

Labyrinths of (Un)consciousness in Hesse's *Steppenwolf*

4.1 Introduction

Kafka's *Prozeß* offers an incisive look into the profound cultural and social issues that would haunt central Europe in the first half of the twentieth century. The analysis of the text shows that the crisis of idealist aesthetics is deeply imbricated with the demise of bourgeois society. Modernization and reification as depicted in *Der Prozeß* transforms human relations in a way that prevents the ideals of the Classical-Romantic tradition from being realized. For all of his differences from Kafka, Hermann Hesse is also aware of the forces corroding the intellectual basis of civilization. In his *Steppenwolf*, the perilous state of German culture is captured by the city labyrinth. But in contrast to Kafka, Hesse clearly identifies with the Classical-Romantic tradition, as evidenced by Haller's references to figures such as Goethe, Novalis, and Bürger. In fact, Hesse seeks new ways of restoring vitality to idealist aesthetics, a goal which at the same time can be seen as a blueprint for molding the fragments of modern society into a dynamic and cohesive totality.

The root cause of the crisis of idealist aesthetics in *Der Steppenwolf* is the tension between nature and spirit, an issue which appears throughout Hesse's oeuvre. In *Siddhartha*, the poles determine two alternative paths of development: Siddhartha devotes himself to religious study in isolation before pursuing sensuous pleasures in society. In *Narziß und Goldmund*, the two contrasting existential possibilities are objictified in the lives of not one but two figures. *Der Steppenwolf* depicts a historical moment when the conflict between spirit and nature assumes its most dangerous forms on an individual as well as on a societal level. The nameless modern city, a product of human civilization, is virtually devoid of nature. On the other hand, modern forms of thought oppress human individuals. In the Magic Theater, Haller echoes the author's hostility towards a particular aspect of the intellect, instrumental reason. The excessive reliance on reason leads to mechanistic social relations, which, in Haller's view, characterize the United States and the Soviet Union. Life in such heartlessly managed societies is devoid of any higher intellectual purpose.

The sundering of the constitutive elements of idealist aesthetics is further exacerbated by the fact that the civilization is caught between two times. As Haller himself observes, the old is breaking down, while the new has not yet been born. Consequently, many wish to return to the ostensible innocence of the pre-war days. The professor, a leading figure in bourgeois culture, is a political reactionary who is a pronounced anti-Communist and has anti-Semitic attitudes. In other words, he rejects some of the most prominent elements of modern cultural and political life. As the car hunt in the Magic Theater reveals, there are others who wish to return to nature as a way of overcoming the oppressive sterility of bourgeois society. But this episode shows that this desire can lead to anarchy, if not the total destruction of civilization.

The cultural crisis is signified by the city labyrinth. In this bleak city, the lonely and anguished Harry Haller struggles to make sense out of his desperate existence. Some critics such as Joseph Mileck,[1] Colin Wilson,[2] George Field,[3] Claude Hill,[4] and Margot Böttcher[5] assert that Haller, much like Hesse himself, is a gifted intellectual and an outsider who is alienated from the petrified world of bourgeois society. At the same time, however, Haller also identifies with bourgeois culture. This contradiction epitomizes his own seemingly hopeless personal crisis and links it to the cultural crisis as depicted in the text. Frequently he despairs of finding the meaning of his tormented existence as he wanders through the city labyrinth. At times, he becomes so depressed about his inner conflicts that he contemplates suicide. Haller's fundamental problem is that he cannot reconcile the wild, passionate wolf in him with the refined, cultivated man. The tension between man (*Geist*) and wolf (*Natur*) tears at the fabric of Haller's personality. In the "Treatise of the Steppenwolf," these two poles are each inserted into extended registers: nature is linked to the realm of the body and the female, while spirit is connected to the mind and the male. This series of polarities points to the underlying Romantic conception of the text. The figure of Haller, a reflective intellectual, begins to fuse these polarities, above all that of spirit and nature, by enjoying bodily experiences. In order to find a meaningful way of living in the world, Haller must undergo the process of individuation, to use Jungian terms. Critics such as Emmanuel Maier,[6] Ludwig Völker,[7] and Edward Timms[8] have pointed out the elements of Jungian psychology in the text. Joseph Mileck argues that the lonely and suicidal Haller is a cipher for Hesse himself. In the early 1920s, Hesse experienced severe depression at the breakup of his second marriage and sought treatment from a Jungian analyst. His desperate emotional state echoes Haller's despondency at the end of his marriage to Erika. Hesse's recovery was aided by frequent visits to the pleasure districts in Zurich. During this period, Hesse associated with young pleasure-seekers who served as a model for the figures of Hermine, Maria, and Pablo (Mileck). In Haller's case, the process of individuation entails achieving an identity as a unique self by going through a process of total personality development. To this end, he must join the pieces of his fragmented psyche into a dynamic totality. A close analysis shows that corporality plays an instrumental role in Haller's development in several crucial respects. Haller cannot affirm life until he acknowledges death, the mortality of his empirical self. The fear of death hinders the development of aspects of his personality. Further, Haller's process of development is aided, if not guided, by figures who are quite literally embodiments of his psyche. To be sure, Hermine, Maria, and Pablo are separate individuals from Haller. But they also allegorically represent parts of Haller's mind.[9] According to Eugen Stelzig,[10] Pablo is Haller's shadow. The shadow, as defined by Jungian theorist M. L. Franz,[11] is an aspect of the psyche which represents the opposite side of the ego and is associated with "just those qualities that one dislikes most in people....If the shadow figure contains valuable, vital forces, they ought to be assimilated into actual experience and not repressed" (von Franz 182-183).

Maria and Hermine have long been identified as Haller's anima. According to Carl Gustav Jung, logic and objective reality prevail in the attitude of the male towards the outside world, whereas the anima is the soul, or the inner attitude towards the unconscious.[12] For men, the anima is female:

> The anima is a personification of all feminine psychological tendencies in a man's psyche, such as vague feelings and moods...receptiveness to the irrational, capacity for personal love, feeling for nature, and...his relation to the unconscious.... (von Franz 186)

Thus, Haller's erotic encounters with these women must also be read as steps towards integrating the anima into his psyche. Haller's desire for the female body enables him to come close to fulfilling his desire for wholeness. In this, an important difference between Hesse's *Steppenwolf* and Kafka's *Prozeß* is revealed. Underlying Kafka's text is a dialectical conception of corporality: the figures can have either an intellectual or a material relationship to the body. In Hesse's *Steppenwolf*, by contrast, the body is the point at which the polarities nature and spirit must be fused. The erotic union with female figures enables Haller to gain profound insights, thereby bringing him closer to his goal of achieving immortality. The body is the crucial link between the Romantic and Jungian elements of Hesse's text. Hesse has a Romantic notion of love, according to which love fuses polarities into a higher unity; there is in this an unmistakable echo of Haller's process of achieving psychic wholeness. In the end, eros opens the way to the Magic Theater.

The Magic Theater labyrinth is the key episode in Haller's development. It is here that Haller develops a new understanding of himself and cultural forces by observing the interplay of nature and spirit on the individual and societal levels. The Magic Theater is in fact an objectification of Haller's mind and is represented by Hesse as a labyrinth. As I will show, this too is congruent with Jungian psychology, in which the unconscious is thought to be symbolized by the labyrinth. Since both the city and Haller's mind are represented as labyrinths, his existential crisis is a metonymy of the cultural crisis. Should Haller develop an interpretation of life, it would perforce represent a new way of reading modern culture. Thus, the outcome of Haller's search for the meaning of life provides information on the possibility of cultural renewal on the basis of idealist aesthetics codes.

4.2 City Labyrinth

Haller is, without any doubt, disoriented in the modern world. His pitiable state is caused in part by the cultural disorientation of the depicted society, a German-speaking country in the turbulent 1920s. The bewildering and hellish nature of the society is signified by the city labyrinth in *Der Steppenwolf*.

The city labyrinth in *Der Steppenwolf* is connected with some of the same motif and thematic patterns that I discussed in section 3.2 of the previous chapter on *Der Prozeß*. The city labyrinth in *Der Steppenwolf* has similar spatial configurations to those in *Der Prozeß*. In both works, nature is virtually absent, a state of affairs that points to the tension between spirit and nature. In both texts, the city is a dark, enclosed space. Haller wanders about the bleak, forbidding city as he ponders his seemingly meaningless existence. The one time Haller moves through the city during the day, he ends up appropriately enough, following a funeral train which seems to him to be as dead as the concrete wasteland which entraps him. But, for the most part, Haller ventures out into the city at night. In order to make his way through the labyrinth, Haller must choose the right way from a number of intersecting paths (streets). The similarity of the paths makes his search for the meaning of life all the more difficult. In the darkness Haller does not recognize a unique building or striking detail that sets one street apart from the rest. No matter which way he turns he ends up going down a dark desolate street that seems to mirror the one he just left. At one point, he observes that buildings on both sides of a street form a cavern, implying that he is in the depths of an abyss. Worse yet, this is Haller's third stay in the city, suggesting that he does not know how to escape from the labyrinth.

The center of the city labyrinth can only be the Black Eagle, where the decisive meeting with Hermine takes place. It is apparent that, with Hermine, Haller traces a path that follows the pattern of the Crane Dance, which was associated with the cycles of nature. For Haller first moves towards death, then reverses his direction and moves towards light, nature, and new life. On the night he meets Hermine, Haller races through the dark city to commit suicide. He actually moves in a spiral pattern towards his apartment. But the fear of death prevents him from taking the final step. On his way, he sees the Black Eagle tavern, to which the mysterious man with the treatise had directed him. There he meets Hermine, who will play an instrumental role in his development. Haller's encounter with her halts his movement to death. She succeeds in turning him in the opposite direction, towards rebirth in a process of growth that culminates in "hell."

One issue common to both texts is reification. Haller contrasts his own attachment to intellectual or spiritual ideals to the fascination of the modern individual with consumer goods. In one of his attacks, he targets the car for a particularly sharp critique:

> Der "moderne" Mensch...liebt die Dinge nicht mehr, nicht einmal sein Heiligstes, sein Automobil, das er baldmöglichst gegen eine bessere Marke hofft tauschen zu können. (Hesse, *GW* 7: 350)

Modern individuals are not so much attached to actual commodities as goods, but as tokens which can be replaced by an even better version. Haller's quote critiques the same logic that Josef K. applies to female helpers in *Der Prozeß*. For Haller, the insipid offerings of modern culture are fitting symbols of this intellectually barren age. He belittles tawdry dance music, mindless radio broadcasts and movies with their contrived plots. Worse yet, the tradition with which Haller identifies has sunk to the depths of triviality, as the sentimental picture of Goethe in the professor's apartment indicates. Berman asserts that in *Der Steppenwolf* Hesse delivers a biting critique of the reification of culture:

> In Hesse's account the reification of established culture encompasses both a monumentalization of the literary legacy and...a mechanization of life forms. Cultural material loses its vitality, just as middle-class normalcy grows increasingly rigid. (189)

The depicted civilization is one that is cut off from the "original creative forces of life" (Berman 190). It is hardly surprising that Haller cannot find his place in the modern world. But the problem for him is that he must look in the city, the epitome of modern civilization, for a more meaningful way of being. The analysis of Haller's movement in the city labyrinth must begin with the house, the starting point of his movements.

4.3 Haller: The Quester Figure

It is fitting that the city is represented as a labyrinth, a mythological underworld, because Haller's miserable existence is for him a kind of living hell. Haller is a sensitive and highly educated intellectual who is alienated from society. An avowed pacifist, Haller admires Ghandi, whose picture hangs in his room. Ghandi's ideals are opposed by the industrialists and reactionary generals whose militaristic politics Haller bitterly denounces in his articles. Haller's writings make him the target of fierce counterattacks in the press. Because of this, Haller can hardly intellectually identify with his contemporaries.

On a more personal level as well, Haller is isolated from the world. There is no mention of friends in the text, save Hermann, his boyhood friend. Haller had conversations with the professor on his first visit to the city, but the two did not stay in contact afterwards. In the "Treatise on the Steppenwolf," Haller's difficulty in establishing friendships is traced back to the divisions in his personality. In Haller's case, other individuals are drawn to the man in him only to be repelled by the wolf, or are attracted to the wolf and are eventually disappointed in the man. By the same token, Haller's internal conflicts prevent him from forming meaningful relationships to others. The nephew of Haller's landlady surmises that this is the legacy of Haller's painful upbringing. He speculates that Haller's parents and teachers tried unsuccessfully to break his will; this childhood ordeal only made Haller hate himself (Hesse, *GW* 7: 191).

It appears that young Haller internalized this conflict with the authority figures from his youth and still cannot overcome it. He suffers from acute conflicts in his personality which prevent him from loving and being loved. The fragmentation of the individual's personality is a characteristic of the theme of the city.[13] Thus, the theme of the city in *Der Steppenwolf* establishes a causal relationship between the destructive forces in the modern world and the personality disorders of individuals.

Haller is not only a deeply troubled individual, but also, and more importantly, the embodiment of German *Geist*, the mind of Germany. While this aspect of the figure of Haller has not attracted much notice in the secondary literature on Hesse, there are in fact a series of reasons that support such an allegorical reading of the figure. Haller, who has works by leading writers from the Enlightenment through Romanticism in his room, is himself an intellectual who composes journalistic pieces and lyric poetry. Haller is therefore a writer who stands in the same tradition as the writers whom he admires. Moreover, the treatise identifies Haller as one of the intellectually gifted few who infuse bourgeois culture with new energy. Two of those figures, Goethe and Mozart, live on as immortals in Haller's mind. Likewise, the Jungian elements in the text support the transindividual composition of the figures. The figures of Maria, Pablo, and Hermine are individuals and at the same time collective archetypes. Further, both the city and Haller's mind (the Magic Theater) are represented as labyrinths; in other words, Haller's mind mirrors the state of civilization (*Geist*).

This level of signification adds another dimension to Haller's quest to find the meaning of life. It is clear that should he find a new understanding of life, he would necessarily have to reinterpret the cultural codes with which he operates. At stake, then, is not only the fate of a depressive intellectual but also that of the bourgeois cultural tradition (*bürgerliche Kultur*) in modern society.

4.4 House

A close analysis of the motif of the house is crucial for illuminating central aspects of Haller's relationship to the world. In *Der Steppenwolf*, as in Kafka's *Prozeß*, the motif of the house provides information on the quester figure's way of being in the world. In *Der Steppenwolf*, the motif of the house has the specific function of furnishing the reader with insights on Haller's relationship to the bourgeois society.

Despite the fact that he relentlessly attacks bourgeois culture and attitudes, Haller consistently takes up residence in middle class homes. Like Josef K., Haller has nearly no contact with the others in the house. Haller has, at most, limited interaction with the landlady and her nephew. By all appearances, Haller is attracted not so much to middle class individuals as to the aura of stability which bourgeois homes exude. As Haller drinks tea with the landlady in her salon, he finds "Großväterbilder" and "Großvätermöbel" beautiful (Hesse, *GW* 7: 290). The term "Großväter" suggest that the decor of the room signifies continuity. Hence, Haller finds signs of the tradition of bourgeois domestic life beautiful. Haller's feeling of security in middle class homes can undoubtedly be ascribed to his memories of his mother and above all to her meticulous care for the home in which he grew up. Haller describes his mother as a "Bürgersfrau" who grew flowers and kept their apartment as neat and orderly as possible. Haller does not, however, mention any sort of emotional warmth for his family.

It is more than a little surprising that Haller, though a vociferous critic of the sterility and intellectual emptiness of bourgeois life, appreciates the punctilious sense of order which he detects in his fellow tenants. He is especially moved by the fact that their devotion to the household includes caring for plants, much as his mother did in his youth. On the stairs, the nephew catches Haller savoring the scent of two plants, the azalea and the Norfolk pine ("Araukarie"), in front of one of the apartments:

> ...der Araukarienplatz hier, der ist so strahlend rein, so abgestaubt und gewichst und abgewaschen, so unantastbar sauber daß es förmlich ausstrahlt. Wie da der Geruch von Bodenwachs und ein schwacher Nachklang von Terpentin zusammen mit dem Mahagoni, den abgwaschenen Pflanzenblättern und allem einen Duft ergibt, einen Superlativ von bürgerlicher Reinheit, von Sorgfalt und Genauigkeit, von Pflichterfüllung und Treue im kleinen. (Hesse, *GW* 7: 195)

Haller's rapturous description of the plants is telling in several respects. Ordinarily, the azalea and Norfolk pine are used in landscaping. Here they are removed from outdoors and he appreciates them as mere decorations which need to be cleaned like a piece of furniture. He enjoys the plants not as part of the natural world but as tokens of the orderly bourgeois world. Thus, Haller's preference for middle class homes is far more than a nostalgic remembrance of his mother. It reflects the fact that Haller is a member of the bourgeois culture which he attacks in his writing. The status of the plants is yet another indication that the depicted civilization (*Geist*) is destroying nature.

By implication, Haller, the representative of German *Geist* does not know how to relate to nature.[14] On an individual level, this means that Haller does not know how to confront the somatic realm. Along these lines, his attitudes are at odds with underlying sensuous needs. This becomes evident when he first examines his new home in the city by sniffing the air. Congruent with this, he later dwells on the "odor" of jazz music, the very form of music which later paves the way for Haller to enjoy long denied sensuous experiences. It is as though the *Natur* aspect of Haller's being resists complete domination and on occasion compels him to change his orientation, as if by picking up the scent to a new form of existence.

It is then Haller's inability to escape the contradictions of bourgeois culture and attitudes which leaves him in a precarious emotional and intellectual state. It is as though he has internalized the logic of a culture which, in a historical context, is on the decline. In the end, he will not be able to resolve the contradictions by remaining within the confines of the middle class world. His attempt to find a way out of the dilemma is represented through his movements from the house to the city. The outcome of Haller's quest to find a more meaningful way of life hinges on his ability to alter his relationship the body.

4.5 Haller's Paths

Clearly, Haller does not find a meaningful way of relating to others in his house. On the contrary, sources of deep conflict in Haller become evident in the analysis of the motif of the house. It is therefore only logical that Haller sets out from the house into the city in search of the meaning of life. In contrast to K., Haller does not have a well-defined pattern of movements. For his trial K. goes to a number of places which mirror the space of his apartment. Haller, on the other hand, spends entire nights aimlessly wandering about the city streets. He does not have a particular destination in mind nor does he go to see anyone since he shuns human contact.

As in *Der Prozeß*, the motif of darkness in *Der Steppenwolf* signifies the quester figure's existential confusion. The motif further signifies the figure's existential dread. As he moves through the city, Haller despairs of the state of his life. He hates his life so much that he considers following the example of Adelbert Stifter by committing suicide. At another point, the thought of killing himself when he turns fifty years old gives him comfort and ameliorates the pain of his troubled life. But Haller cannot bring himself to take the final step. In addition, the theme of dread appears in conjunction with the theme of aggression. On the night on which Haller visits the professor, he berates the latter's picture of Goethe, and in so doing, offends the professor and his wife. Haller subsequently leaves and moves through the dark city towards his apartment where he intends to put an end to his life. Thus, in both *Der Prozeß* and *Der Steppenwolf*, the motif of darkness occurs with dread and aggression. It is true that K. has a material orientation in life while Haller has an intellectual one. In spite of this difference, there is an underlying commonality with respect to the motif of darkness. In both texts, the motif indicates that the figure's existential confusion stems from not knowing how to relate to corporality.

Haller can only gain some degree of relief from his situation by going to a concert or tavern. In fact, concerts and taverns are the only stopping points mentioned on Haller's early movements. His response to a beautiful piece of classical music reveals that an integral element of his existential crisis is the disparity between his ideals and the state of his own life. As I will point out, Haller himself later reads the ideal-real polarity in terms of the spirit-nature polarity. He metaphorically describes his miserable existence in spatial terms. For Haller, hearing a beautiful piece of music tears down the walls of his everyday existence. Momentarily freed from the real world, he traverses the shining golden path to the immortals:

> da war zwischen zwei Takten eines Holzbläsers gespielten Piano mir plötzlich wieder die Tür zum Jenseits aufgegangen, ich hatte Himmel durchflogen und Gott an der Arbeit gesehen.... (Hesse, *GW* 7: 210)

The experience of listening to this beautiful work is so exhilarating that Haller has a vision of a door opening to the path to the divine. The motif cluster path-door-light, a central configuration in *Der Prozeß*, will recur frequently in *Der Steppenwolf* as well, but for now, it cannot be overlooked that the shining path to God exists only in Haller's mind. He cannot, however, find such a path in the real world, as his reference to the dirt and filth reveal.

After this exalted moment at the concert, Haller contents himself with a visit to the tavern. As he drinks wine, he longingly reflects on the music which had just enthralled him. He hopes that the divine spirit of the music has left seeds in his soul which will one day become a beautiful flower. By implication, the immortals have already achieved the synthesis of spirit and nature. In Haller's case, the two poles are in conflict. When he initially heard the music, he described how it tore down walls, in other words, how it destroyed civilization. The juxtaposition of nature (flower) and civilization (walls) expresses a conflict in the figure which almost amounts to a wish to destroy civilization. This configuration establishes a connection between dread and aggression that is present in Kakfa's *Prozeß*.

The names of the taverns which Haller frequents point to the grave political implications of Haller's thinking. The first two taverns mentioned by name are "Zum Schwarzen Adler" and the "Stahlhelm." The black eagle and the steel helmet are two patriotic symbols, tokens of the reactionary, militaristic forces Haller criticizes in the press. That Haller never reflects on these names indicates that he is unaware of his latent kinship with his political foes. The black eagle is also reminiscent of the large heraldic bird above the doorway to Demian's house in Hesse's *Demian* (1919).[15] The symbol of the bird is, according to Timms, encoded in Jungian terms (169, 171). In *Demian*, the bird is struggling out of the egg which represents the world. "Wer geboren werden will, muß eine Welt zerstören. Der Vogel fliegt zu Gott..." (Hesse, *GW* 5: 91). This echoes Haller's apparent wish to tear down the walls of civilization, a wish which makes the hidden danger in Haller become all too clear. Taken to their conclusion, Haller's thoughts reveal a desire to destroy the real world in order to achieve an ideal form of existence. But this desire aligns Haller with the political reactionaries who, as the configurations in the two novels indicate, respond to the cultural crisis by pursuing an aggressive agenda of destroying the old world in order to construct a new one of their own.

4.6 Path-Door-Light

In the initial stages of his search for the meaning of life, Haller wanders through the darkness of the city labyrinth. His movements in the space of the labyrinth can for the most part be broken down into a repeated series of the motif cluster path-darkness. But through an hallucination, the figure expands his pattern of movements to the configuration path-door-light. Haller imagines that he sees an illuminated sign flashing in the old city. He gains valuable knowledge by moving towards the light; he obtains the treatise of the

Steppenwolf.

It is fitting that Haller, who once glimpsed God in his vision at the concert, is lead by an hallucination to the wisdom of the immortals. Haller sees the mysterious sign advertising the Magic Theater. The sign flashes above a door in the wall. He tries unsuccessfully to open the door. In effect, he has run into a dead end, comprised of a church and a hospital, one a place of healing for the soul, the other one for the body. Significantly, the light flashes outside both buildings. Moreover, the church is shrouded in darkness. This implies that Haller's path of self-realization leads him away from traditional institutions which together form a barrier. Since he cannot extend his path through the door, he must content himself with the treatise. This analysis of his personality functions as light from the immortals. Only the immortals have the perspective to compose a treatise with such insight.[16] In terms of the pattern of door-light, it is a new glimpse of the eternal realm at the end of the path.

The difference between the central texts in *Der Prozeß* (the parable) and *Der Steppenwolf* (the treatise) is striking. In Kafka's *Prozeß*, the parable concerns the failure of the individual to find the meaning of life. The spectrum of interpretations of the parable reflect the crisis in the cultural tradition. The various interpreters cannot say what the failure of the man actually means. Consequently, interpreters have enormous difficulty applying the lessons of the parable to individual cases. By contrast, the treatise in Hesse's *Steppenwolf* already is an interpretation of *one particular* individual, Haller.

The treatise contains insights needed for Haller to reorient himself in life. Given the focus on the nature-spirit polarity in the treatise, it is a product of Classical-Romantic tradition. Underlying the analysis of Haller's personality in the treatise is the notion that the cause of his existential crisis is the tension between these poles. According to the treatise, the human individual is a bridge between nature and spirit (Hesse, *GW* 7: 245). Nature is the "Urmutter," while spirit is the "Urvater" of the individual. In Haller's case, there is a struggle between the female-nature pole and its male-spiritual counterpart. He owes the civilized, cultured, and divine ("Göttlich") side of personality to his paternal blood and the wild, passionate, and devilish traits to his maternal blood (Hesse, *GW* 7: 226). This emotive, female *Natur* element in Haller's personality can, in terms of idealist aesthetics, be read as the realm of the body: the treatise identifies "Natur" with Haller's wolf aspect, "Unschuld" and "Triebleben" (Hesse, *GW* 7: 247). It is the unresolved conflict between spirit and nature, the somatic domain, which causes dread in Haller;

"zwischen beiden Mächten schwankt angstvoll bebend sein Leben" (Hesse, *GW* 7: 245).

In a sense, Haller's embodiment is a painful reminder of his existential guilt, his incompleteness. In the Magic Theater, his friend Gustav the theologian attributes his own guilt to the fact that he was born. As the treatise points out, birth is the moment at which he was separated from the immortals. To use Heideggerian terms, Haller was thrown (*geworfen*) at birth from the divine realm into the real world, where, in contrast to the immortals, he exists as an embodied mortal subject. In this context, the implications of Haller's suicidal tendencies become clear. They stem from a desire to destroy his mortal empirical self so that he can escape the guilt of being and return in spirit to the immortals. He is, to quote the treatise, one of those who is afflicted with guilt feelings caused by the process of individuation. But the treatise states that he can only reach the immortals by undergoing a process of continual transformation. This in no way is a call to return to a naive, innocent state of being. Rather, it necessitates immersing oneself in the guilt involved in the painful ordeal of becoming human (*Menschwerdung*), a process which entails recognizing his thousands of existential possibilities and integrating them into a harmonious unity in his soul.

Given the link between guilt and corporality, this implies that sensuous experiences are an integral part of the process of becoming. Along these lines, Haller observes in the Magic Theater that eros had long produced feelings of guilt in him. Moreover, an analysis of Hesse's essay "Gedanken zu Dostojewskys Idiot"[17] reveals that the realm of the body (*Tier* or, more generally, nature) offers new possibilities for human development. Hesse views Myshkin as a model in that he shows the way that each individual must go:

> ...das Annehmen des Chaos, Rückkehr ins Ungeordnete, Rückweg ins Unbewußte, ins Gestaltlose, ins Tier...Rückkehr zu allen Anfängen. Nicht um dort zu bleiben, nicht um Tier...zu werden, sondern um uns neu zu orientieren, um an den Wurzeln unseres Seins vergessene Triebe und Entwicklungsmöglichkeiten aufzufinden, um aufs neue Schöpfung, Wertung, Teilung der Welt vornehmen zu können. (Hesse, *GDI* 223)

This quote echoes the statement in the treatise that Haller "...müßte tief in das Chaos der eigenen Seele blicken und zum vollen Bewußtsein seiner selbst kommen" (Hesse, *GW* 7: 238). In the quote from the essay, the

"Rückweg ins Tier" is an obvious reference to the sensuous *Natur* aspect of humanity. The realm of the body is linked to the unconscious and sensuous drives which are a vital force for creating a new world. The key to this process is the establishment of a new value system, a value system capable of revitalizing European civilization which had been devastated by cataclysmic events in the early twentieth century. Indeed, Hesse apparently believes that the exploration of repressed drives can lead to a kind of a spiritual renewal of the both individual and European culture since he likens Myshkin to Christ. Hence, Hesse effectively turns idealist aesthetics on its head in this passage. It is not in the ordering powers of reason or the intellect but in the chaos of the unconscious that meaningful values for human existence can be found. In Haller's case, eros, the desire for the (female) body, gives him access to his unconscious, through which he gains the awareness to reorient himself in the world.

But as Haller reads the treatise, it is still not at all clear that he will find his way out of his predicament. Moreover, Haller would have to take new paths in the city labyrinth in order to apply the lessons of the treatise. He would have to seek out individuals with whom he could have the sensuous experiences which would give new meaning to his life. Thus, Haller's progress in the city labyrinth will hinge on his ability to redefine his relationship to the body in the way delineated in the treatise.

4.7 Crane Dance: Path to New Life

With the receipt of the treatise, Haller has the insight necessary to change his life, but there is still no sign that he is committed to undergoing a new process of development. He does not begin to apply the lessons of the treatise to his own life until he gets to know Hermine. With her help, Haller manages to reorient himself in the labyrinth as he begins to move towards light and new life.

Haller's reversal of direction on the decisive night with Hermine can easily been seen as a kind of Crane Dance pattern, the dance which celebrated Theseus's successful movement through the labyrinth. Haller moves towards death, stops, and reverses his direction. He then begins to move on the path to nature and new life. Appropriately enough, Haller's day begins when he ventures out into the city, where he joins a funeral train. The funeral itself only reinforces Haller's conviction of the senselessness of modern life. By the end of the evening, Haller is ready to put an end to his own life.

For Haller, the episode with the professor signals that he has no hope of reconciling the two antagonistic halves of the Steppenwolf.

In a fit of depression, he makes his way back through the dark city to his apartment, where he intends to kill himself. He actually moves in a spiral path, the pattern of the Crane Dance, towards death. Haller moves in a series of circles as he approaches the center, death. But he stops this centripetal movement when he sees the Black Eagle. Inside, he discovers Hermine. It is she who enables Haller to reorient himself in the labyrinth and, on an allegorical plane, in life. Not only does her care dissuade him from killing himself, but she also takes him on paths which lead to jazz bars where he enjoys the sensuous experiences necessary for his personal growth.

For his part, Haller immediately realizes that he needs her. Though she is a bargirl, she can actually be viewed as the personification of the divine spirit expressed in ethereal music. During his rapturous moment at the concert, he described his life in spatial terms: the music tore down the walls of his existence and opened up the shining path to God. In the Black Eagle, the figure of Haller continues this metaphorical chain by extending it to Hermine. He actually likens her to a door and light in his dark, constricted life:

> Plötzlich eine Tür offen, durch die das Leben zu mir hereinkam....
> (Hesse, *GW* 7: 288)
> Sie war...das winzige lichte Loch in meiner Angsthöhle. Sie war die Erlösung, der Weg ins Freie. (Hesse, *GW* 7: 292)

The full significance of Hermine's impact on him can be grasped if these spatial metaphors are applied to the space of the city labyrinth. I am referring specifically to the old city, the one place in the city where Haller sees the light, the flashing sign advertising the Magic Theater. It is here that the motif of the path is expanded into the configuration path-door-light. Haller's description of Hermine effectively defines her as the recurrence of that same motif cluster. But in the old city, Haller comes to a dead end, whereas here Hermine leads him down the path to light in the Magic Theater.

Eventually, she takes Haller on a new path in the city. This path to the light and new life must be understood as the second leg of the Crane Dance. In the ancient world, this dance was used to celebrate the cycles of nature. Likewise, Haller begins to move to new places in which the motif of the flower appears. It is little wonder that plants are significant for the figure since, as I pointed out earlier, he sits transfixed as he enjoys the scent of the azalea and the Norfolk pine. But it is the flower, not dusted and polished house plants, that rejuvenate Haller. The motif of the flower encompasses actual plants and the spirit of the immortals. Hermine appears with flowers; she has a flower in her hair when Haller first meets her and there is a vase with orchids on the table when the two get together the following week. The flower in Hermine's hair is not the only one Haller sees in the Black Eagle. In Haller's dream, Goethe undergoes continual transformation. As the old poet dances, even the medals on his chest turn into flowers. Similarly, Haller begins to glimpse the spirit of the immortals by enjoying the dancing with women.

Congruent with this, the motif of the flower has a second variation: women. Haller compares Hermine, Maria, and the women at the masked ball to flowers. Of all of the women, Maria does the most to help regenerate the long dormant *Natur* aspect of his being. Haller actually calls her a flower and "drinks her youth" on their first night of passion. In a sense, the flower provides Haller with the fresh nectar of spring which enables him to undergo a new process of development. This experience with her enables him, the representative of *Geist*, to have his first vision of nature. The motif of the flower is expanded to include the natural landscapes in his visions. Summoned by eros, the important people of his life appear as a beautiful landscape. Subsequently, the loves of his life appear in a series like delicate fragrant flowers (Hesse, *GW* 7: 330).

But on the fateful night at the Black Eagle, Haller is still a long way from finding the meaning of life. His development will proceed in a series of tests. Each time, he will have to choose between crossing through a doorway to continue on the path to nature, or retreating into the darkness on his former paths. Haller can only enjoy a new life by making a series of movements to jazz clubs in which the configuration path-door-flower (young women) appears. This series of movements, a crucial stage in Haller's personality development, is not composed of a repetition of the same event. Rather, each movement marks a higher stage in his ability to love. I must therefore focus on the role of love in Haller's development as he moves through the city labyrinth.

4.8 Path-Door-Flower

So far, I have pointed out that the encounter with Hermine is literally a turning point for Haller. In a process which corresponds to the pattern of the Crane Dance, Haller halts his spiral-like movement towards death and reverses direction. This path is the path to nature; congruent with this, Haller must make a series of movements in the city labyrinth in which the configuration path-door-flower occurs. If Haller can continue on the path, he could potentially traverse the labyrinth and find a meaningful form of life.

At this point, the analysis of Haller's development must turn to the means by which he undergoes his regeneration: his capacity to love. Haller makes progress on his new path, the second half of the Crane Dance, to the extent that his ability to love grows. In Hesse's *Steppenwolf*, love enables the quester figure to move through the labyrinth towards light and new life. In *Der Prozeß*, K.'s uncontrollable desire for the flesh precludes any intellectual exchange that might give him insight into his situation. In Haller's case however, erotic desire does not exacerbate the mind-body tension, but actually paves the way to resolving this tension. The function of love in the text can be traced back to the Classical-Romantic codes with which Hesse operates. Underlying Haller's development is the Romantic notion that love can trigger an expansion of the self. In general, leading Romantic thinkers strived to fuse existential opposites into a new and dynamic totality. Among the most important polarities for them are the individual and the universal, humanity and God, and spirit and nature. For Schleiermacher, love is the drive to perceive the individual and knowledge of the individual is an organ for knowing the universe.[18] Intuition has as its precondition "...eine Einheit von Körper- und Geisteswelt..." (Kluckhohn 454). Schleiermacher radicalizes the concept of Platonic love in connecting the sex drive with spiritual needs (Kluckhohn 453-454). For this reason, the physical union of man and woman, "organic opposites," is a highly ethical act which results in "eine absolute Verschmelzung des Bewußtseins" (Kluckhohn 455). According to Schelling, the essence of the human soul is love (Kluckhohn 527). Love connects the soul to God, who is eternal love and nature, since love is also the "Gesamtleben der Natur" (Kluckhohn 526, 528). Love then joins humanity with both God and nature. By implication, love could help Haller find his way back to the divine realm which he glimpsed during the concert.

In this context, corporality plays a twofold role. Clearly, Romantic love implies a more sensuous form of bodily experience for Haller than has previously been the case. Second, the individuals from whom Haller learns to love, Hermine, Maria, and Pablo, are themselves allegorical embodiments of elements of Haller's psyche. I suggest that the Romantic and Jungian elements should be considered as mutually supporting. According to both philosophies, each individual is unique but possesses timeless human qualities that all others share. Further, the conceptions of the figures correspond to

Novalis's idea of the divine, primordial image in all people, an idea present in *Heinrich von Ofterdingen* (Kluckhohn 480). Thus, the process by which Haller strives to achieve psychic wholeness through love can simultaneously be seen in terms of the Romantic notion of joining polarities in a higher unity. This is not to say that Haller's process of development is without difficulties or moments when he is on the verge of regressing into his personal crisis. Haller's transformation is inconceivable without the intervention of Hermine, who nurtures and at times cajoles him. It is surely no coincidence that Hermine, Haller's anima, mothers him, because in Jungian theory, the mother of the individual man forms the character of the anima (von Franz 186). The description of an unhealthy anima figure reads like an analysis of Haller's condition before meeting Hermine: "If he feels that his mother had a negative influence on him his anima will often express itself in irritable, depressed moods, uncertainty, insecurity and touchiness" (von Franz 186). When he first meets Hermine, Haller laments the fact that his strict parents forbade him from enjoying himself or from dancing. Instead, they forced him to learn academic subjects such as Greek and Latin. Congruent with her role as Haller's anima, Hermine treats him like a lost little boy and teaches him to dance. It is significant that an integral element of Haller's rejuvenation is dancing. Dancing was part of the ancient rites which celebrated the successful movement of Theseus through the labyrinth.

As Haller awkwardly stumbles through the moves, it is as though he is again learning how to walk. Haller is effectively cast into the role of a child who is still dependent on his mother. At this stage, Haller can only receive motherly love. Hermine's instruction prepares Haller to enjoy the sensuous pleasures that his parents had denied Haller in his youth. Appropriately enough, the motif cluster path-door-flower occurs as Hermine teaches him dance steps in his room. The new direction in Haller's life is signalled by the flowers which replace the books on the table in the middle of the room; it is a clear sign that the female *Natur* aspect of Haller's being is beginning to emerge.

The next step for Haller is to move to clubs, tokens of modern culture in the city which he had once shunned. He enters through doors into establishments whose names indicate wholeness: Hotel Balance and "Globussäle." The motif of the flower recurs as well in the form of the young women who dance enthusiastically inside. But Haller initially reverts to his old "Steppenwolf" self. He again experiences his usual contempt for the shallow and tawdry pleasures at the jazz club. Hermine becomes angry with him because she recognizes that he is trying to rationalize his fear of asking attractive young women to dance. In the end, however, Hermine prevails on him to approach Maria. To Haller's surprise, Maria agrees to dance with him.

In section 4.7, I identified Maria with the motif of the flower and, more specifically, as the provider of the nectar which rejuvenates Haller. The process of rejuvenation begins on this night and is represented as a bodily transformation. Haller is a gout-stricken man of fifty who previously limped up the stairs to his room. During his dance lessons with Hermine, he struggled to concentrate on making the right steps. With Maria, he dances as smoothly as if he had the body of an athletic man of twenty. Together they form such an agile pair that Haller moves without having to think of the rules he has learned the previous week. Gradually they draw closer and closer to each other until they are almost joined together. The erotic overtones of their dance point to another aspect of corporality. For Haller the aim of dancing is "to overcome the rigid mind-body dualism by putting him in touch with the libidinous energies dammed up within his physical self" (Timms 177). The dance foreshadows their later sexual union.

Haller is not entirely at ease with the changes in his life. Ironically, the next intersection in the labyrinth turns out to be at his own bedroom door. There he could either take the path back to being a depressive intellectual or the path to more sensuous experiences than the ones he has enjoyed to this point. One night, he goes to the cathedral for a performance of spiritual music; the allusion to Haller's return to *Geist* could hardly be more explicit. On his way back to his apartment, Haller bemoans the seemingly chaotic state of his life since the time when he started going to jazz clubs. This moment of reflection parallels his initial unwillingness to dance on his first night out with Hermine. When he returns to his apartment, he detects a strange odor, and actually hesitates at his bedroom door. He could potentially move in another direction, but instead he goes in, and takes the path to nature (motif of the flower). Inside Haller discovers Maria. Their sleeping together represents a Romantic joining of polarities: *Geist-Natur* (motif of the flower), and male-female. For Haller, her caress is not a dissonant coda to the religious music but "...sie waren ihr würdig und ihre Erfüllung" (Hesse, *GW* 7: 326). Haller once remarks that German intellectuals love music so much that they do not understand the world. At this moment, life complements art for the representative of the German mind.

In addition, the night with Maria is a crucial step towards integrating the anima into his psyche. Maria must be considered part of the Hermine-anima figure for two reasons. First, Hermine gives him Maria as a present. Second,

Maria has enjoyed carnal love with Hermine in the past. Both women reinvigorate Haller by leading him to the realm of vision. By sleeping with Maria, Haller has a vision, an episode which corresponds to Myshkin's plunge into chaos. One of the functions of the anima is to put "...a man's mind in tune with the right inner values...thereby opening the way into more profound inner depths" (von Franz 193). In Jungian theory, a physical experience with the female anima figure can revitalize the male, for "...to enter her, i.e. the womb, is to enter the prenatal realm of the unconscious and to be reborn."[19] Thus, this movement on the path to the flower represents progression in Haller's ability to love. With Hermine, he had received a kind of parental love and now he shares in erotic love with Maria. The next occurrence of the path-door-flower configuration takes place when Haller gets to know the musician Pablo. It may at first glance seem contradictory to discuss Pablo in this context since I defined not men but women as a variation of the motif of the flower. Nevertheless, Pablo must be linked with the motif of the flower. First, in the Magic Theater Pablo appears as Mozart, one of the immortals who are linked to the motif of the flower. Second, Pablo offers to make love to both Maria and a shocked Haller. By accepting this proposal, Haller could potentially enjoy the pleasure of the flower while simultaneously sleeping with a female and a male figure. The connection between Pablo and the flower does not stop there. Pablo is a wood-wind player just like the one whose piano playing enthralled Haller at the performance of classical music. After that concert, Haller hoped that the performance will leave seeds in his soul which will one day grow into flowers.

Additionally, Pablo symbolizes an element of Haller's shadow. The shadow is an aspect of the psyche which represents the opposite side of the ego and embodies "just those qualities that one dislikes most in people" (von Franz 182). Haller is at first suspicious of the seemingly inarticulate Pablo and cannot fathom why Hermine would spend a minute with such a shallow, simplistic cad. Haller, however, stands to profit from exchanging ideas with Pablo and sharing in his wild lifestyle. Indeed, Pablo has crucial lessons for Haller. Pablo gives him an example of a higher stage of love: caritas, a kind of committed concern for the plight of others. Haller accompanies him to the apartment of the sick musician Agostino whom Pablo actually nurses. The name Agostino is a clear reference to St. Augustine who was instrumental in defining Christian caritas. All love, Augustine believes, is based on desire. The desire in cupiditas unites people with temporal things. The desire in caritas unites them with God and the eternal world.[20] The difference is essentially their object. Caritas is loving God in one's neighbor while cupiditas is directed at transitory objects. In this context, it is fitting that Pablo himself is an immortal.

Pablo also shares his views on music with a skeptical Haller. From Pablo's statements we can conclude that dance music is the fusion of the *Natur-Geist* polarity on the artistic level. Haller, who cherishes only the works of the great classical composers, encounters a radically different view from his own on what constitutes good music. Pablo explains that the essential value of the Shimmy is the joy and energy it gives listeners. In short, Haller extols the spirit of the great composers expressed in music, while Pablo defends the enthusiasm (*Be-geist-erung*) any kind of music produces in the audience. In effect, Pablo, too, defends the spirit of music, namely the spirit it awakens among dancers who respond in a sensuous way. Pablo's comments echo the view that Goethe expresses in Haller's dream at the Black Eagle.

In the context of the cultural crisis depicted in *Der Steppenwolf*, Pablo and Goethe delineate a form of cultural renewal. Haller, as German *Geist*, seems intent on preserving the intellectual content of artistic artifacts, but at the cost of isolating them from the world in which those works were created. Haller's attitude eventually results in the petrification of the cultural tradition. Pablo and Goethe, however, suggest that the cultural tradition can continue to be a vital force if people have a sensuous experience of the spirit in art. In the Magic Theater the Mozart-Pablo figure at the chessboard explains that play, the core essence of art according to Schiller, is the means of reconstructing the human personality. At this point, Haller's reservations about Pablo's ideas and occasional regression into his Steppenwolf self indicate that he has not yet found a new understanding of life in the modern world. He must therefore enter the labyrinthine Magic Theater in order to develop an interpretation of life, an interpretation which will simultaneously be a reinterpretation of the idealist aesthetic codes with which he operates.

4.9 Magic Theater Labyrinth

While Haller admits that he benefits from dancing and his amorous encounters with Maria, he also knows that they do not satisfy his longing to find the meaning of life. They are merely "Augenblicksfreude." Haller's process of development ultimately leads to his movement through the Magic Theater. The personal and intellectual growth of the figure can be tracked in the course of events at the masked ball and in the Magic Theater by following the recurrence and expansion of the thematic patterns of Haller's development. More specifically, the motifs of love, the path, and the flower deserve close scrutiny in this decisive phase of Haller's regeneration.

Additionally, the Magic Theater, a metaphor for Haller's mind, is a variation of the motif of the labyrinth. I will explore the details which support this representation of the Magic Theater. For now, I will concentrate on the function of the Magic Theater for the text as a whole. As Haller moves through the Magic Theater, he sees how cultural forces, unconscious drives, and his own past experiences shaped his personality. The Magic Theater labyrinth is the a model for (self-)reflection; this function of the labyrinth explains the presence of numerous mirrors in the hallways of the Magic Theater. Hence, the Magic Theater corresponds to the hermeneutical labyrinth in *Der Prozeß*. In both cases, the quester must find orientation in an intellectual labyrinth in order to understand life. The intellectual labyrinth is not coterminous with the labyrinth in the real world, the city. Rather, if the questers find their way through the intellectual labyrinth, they will be prepared to enjoy a more meaningful existence in the real world. If they can apply the insights from their reflection to their lives in modern society, the figures effectively present a solution to the cultural crisis.

In the beginning, it almost appears that Haller might not go to the ball at all. The thought of attending the dance fills him with unease, and he retraces the paths which he took as a Steppenwolf, i.e., before reading the treatise. These paths lead, as noted earlier, to the darkness which signifies Haller's intellectual confusion. Haller stops for a brief visit to the Steel Helmet tavern before going to join the dancers enjoying the jazz music. His subsequent movement to the ball is therefore a recurrence of the second stage of the Crane Dance (4.7); but Haller shows little interest in the festivities. He sits alone in a corner and disparages the exuberant dancers as he wallows in his foul mood. This sequence mirrors that of his first night out with Hermine, (see 4.8) when he at first shied away from dancing. On both occasions, she succeeds in inducing him to dance. At the Masked Ball, she has Haller notified that she awaits him downstairs in "hell." Filled with a rush of anticipation, he enthusiastically dances as he makes his way downstairs.

With Hermine's encouragement, Haller experiences an expansion of his capacity for love. Hermine of course plays an instrumental role in awakening Haller's ability to love; she becomes a mother figure for him and provides him with Maria. In both cases, Haller is attracted to female figures. In the Magic Theater, however, Hermine is dressed as the boy Hermann, Haller's friend from his youth. Haller's love for both the male and female side of the figure is a metonymy for love's fusing polarities into a higher unity. This is in fact the very topic which Hermine discusses with Haller.

The content of the conversation anticipates the all-encompassing love to which Hermine introduces him. Previously, Haller had danced almost exclusively with Maria. But now, Hermine teaches him the way to seduce nearly all the women at the ball. Once again, the young women with whom he dances are described as flowers ("Blüte") (Hesse, *GW* 7: 359). His dancing marks a recurrence of the motif cluster path (to hell)-flower. Haller becomes so intoxicated by eros and the joy of the dance that he experiences a mystical union with the other guests. Critics have suggested that Haller's intoxication enables him to overcome the *principium individuationis* in the Magic Theater (Ziolkowski 221). This corresponds to Nietzsche's notion of the Dionysian, according to which licentiousness is a means of celebrating the unity of all individuals.

Indeed, a transformation occurs in both Hermine and Haller by the end of the ball. His mystical union echoes Hesse's own reading of Myshkin's mystical moment when he can see, feel, and experience everything in the world. Congruent with this, Haller now feels like a part of everyone including the men. This is a significant step beyond the previous pattern of development in two respects. His desire is no longer directed solely at figures who represent parts of his psyche. Rather, for the first time, he believes that he is in all people, even though he was an isolated, alienated outsider only weeks earlier. Second, the identity of the men must not be overlooked. At the beginning of the ball, Haller notes that many are politicians, journalists, and industrialists, the very figures whom he attacks in his articles. Now, however, it is as though Haller, the representative of German *Geist*, has recognized his Romantic image, to use Novalis's term, in the leading members of modern society. In a sense, his soul has been enlarged to the point where it encompasses limitless human possibilities, as the treatise had explained to Haller. This suggests that Haller could give intellectual direction and guidance to modern industrial society on the basis of the Romantic tradition, should he succeed in finding the meaning of life. Along these lines, Berman argues that Hesse describes a kind of mystical or religious experience in which a new type of individual and a new sort of "social bond" come into being at the ball (194).

To find the meaning of life, he must enter his unconscious in the manner which Hesse describes in "Gedanken zu Dostoiewskis Idiot." This is a movement back "ins Tier," into the realm of the body. Along these lines, Hermine reappears at the end of the dance dressed as a woman. For Haller, she embodies all of the women in whom he has fallen in love at the dance.

At this point, she can be seen as *das ewig Weibliche*, a cipher for *Natur*, or of all female qualities in humanity. At the end of the ball, Haller's erotic desire has the same function that it has on his first night with Maria (4.8); it opens up the realm of vision in his mind.

In the end, Pablo enables both Hermine and Haller to enter the Magic Theater. Pablo gives them both hallucinogenic drugs to prepare them for the Magic Theater, whereupon the two figures go into opposite sides of the theater. In Haller's movement into the Magic Theater, the configurations of path-door-light recur. In the old city, Haller sees a strange sign flashing. As he sits with Hermine and Pablo, Haller sees light streaming into the room; clearly, Haller is about to move on the path to the light. The treatise which he obtains in the old city explains how he can gain self-understanding by gazing into the soul. Here, Haller enters the Magic Theater, a metaphor for his unconscious. In other words, he has the chance to achieve self- and world-understanding in essentially the same manner as Prince Myshkin.

There are several compelling reasons for viewing the Magic Theater as a labyrinth. By meeting the others in "hell," Haller moves in a space where the two other main figures are Dionysus (Pablo) and Aphrodite (Hermine), who appear in some versions of the myth of Theseus. The hedonistic Pablo is the embodiment of the Dionysian spirit. At the ball Haller feels the power of Hermine's "hermaphroditic magic." The hermaphroditic figure in Greek mythology is the union of the male Hermes with the female Aphrodite, who is related to the Ariadne figure. Moreover, von Franz argues that the unconscious is often symbolized by "corridors, labyrinths and mazes" (177). Certainly, the hallways and stairs which Haller must traverse to reach Hermine supports this reading. The Magic Theater is in fact a maze-like structure. In the Magic Theater, the main path is a hallway with numerous intersecting paths whose boundaries are marked by doors. Behind the doors are unforeseeable experiences which objectify the manifold aspects of Haller's soul; it is as though his thousands of existential possibilities mentioned in the treatise have each been given a separate room in the Magic Theater.

Hence, there is a labyrinth both in the physical space of the city and in the mental space of Haller's mind. The mirroring of the city and Haller's psyche suggests a correspondence between the people at the ball with whom Haller is mystically united and countless mirror images of Haller in the Magic Theater. The mirror images reappear in varied form as the game pieces at "Aufbau der Persönlichkeit," where the Pablo-gameplayer recapitulates the main arguments of the treatise on reconstructing the human personality. Haller could potentially enhance the consciousness of the others, many of whom guide the cultural life of modern society, by discovering how the various elements of his soul can be joined into a dynamic totality. Central aspects of Haller's psyche are illuminated in the main scenes in the Magic Theater: these scenes deal with diverse aspects of the nature-spirit polarity, the cornerstone of idealist aesthetics.

Thus, in order to achieve wholeness, Haller must understand the role of corporality in his own development and its impact on the cultural codes which have shaped his mind. Two episodes, "Steppenwolfdressur" and "Alle Mädchen sind dein," objectify the relationship of Haller as an individual to nature. The scene in the "Steppenwolfdressur" focuses on Haller's chronic problem, the conflict between man and wolf. At first, the animal tamer forces the wolf to repress its wild nature and to act almost human in a humiliating power struggle. The roles are then reversed as the wolf assumes the dominant position and forces the man to behave like an animal. In this sequence, the motif of food, a prominent motif in Kafka's *Prozeß*, appears in *Der Steppenwolf* as well. Through this demeaning deadlock, the man and the wolf deny each other needed sustenance. The animal tamer has the emaciated wolf play with a rabbit and a lamb. As a reward for his docility, the wolf is given chocolate. In return, the wolf exacts a steep price. The man must resist the caresses of an alluring young woman and chase her away by baring his teeth at her. Finally, the man kills and devours the rabbit.

But Haller is able to satisfy his hunger after opening the door with the sign "Alle Mädchen sind dein." Inside, Haller is returned to his youth when he has a kind of sexual awakening. His "Hunger des Geschlechtes" is momentarily abated when he chews on a spring blossom. The connection between the motif of the flower and women is reestablished as Rosa Kreisler, his first love, appears. The connection is in fact reinforced by her first name. Haller is initially torn between his desire and the feelings of guilt which love produces in him, but in contrast to the real life experiences of his youth, he overcomes his sense of guilt and approaches the young woman. Rosa is only the first of a series of young women with whom Haller enjoys erotic encounters; he has amorous experiences with all the women to whom he had ever been attracted. Haller's immersion into carnal pleasures actually propels him on his way to the immortals. After having a vision of God at the concert, Haller had hoped that seeds of the divine might one day bloom in him. Now, that very wish seems to be fulfilled: "...alle versäumte Liebe meines Lebens blühte in dieser Traumstunde zauberhaft in meinem Garten..." (Hesse, *GW* 7: 396). Further, Haller describes his erotic encounters as a "a river of temptation." This formulation echoes the words of the treatise, which states that all of creation is "cast into the dirty river of becoming" (Hesse, *GW* 7: 247). In the treatise, Haller is also urged to immerse himself "immer weiter in die Schuld, immer tiefer in die Menschwerdung" in order to become immortal. The term becoming *Werden* connects the metaphor of the stream with the idea of guilt, and both of these terms are associated with love in this scene in the Magic Theater.

The fact that Haller does not hesitate to explore these two sections of the Magic Theater reveals a fundamental difference between Haller and Josef K. in Kafka's *Prozeß*. In contrast to K., Haller is willing to extend his path in the labyrinth by going through doors and confronting his guilt. K. becomes hopelessly lost in the hermeneutical labyrinth as he cannot make sense of the interpretations of the parable. This illustrates his failure to engage the cultural tradition. Haller, on the other hand, moves through the Magic Theater labyrinth and enters two scenes which force him to confront cultural forces. In his visit with Mozart and in the car hunt, Haller is shown desperate attempts to redeem humanity by expiating guilt, human incompleteness, on a cultural plane. The Pablo-Mozart figure takes Haller to a theater where they watch Brahms and Wagner leading trains of followers in the desert. The scene is reminiscent of the movie which Haller sees on his way to the ball, the depiction of Moses leading his people out of Egypt. To his horror, Haller sees himself carrying books and wandering aimlessly in the desert with Wagner and Brahms. As he watches with Mozart he is appalled that Adam and original sin are there as well. All four figures Moses, Brahms, Wagner, and Haller try to give guidance to society in order to address the consequences of original sin. Traversing the barren desert suggests that there is a common pattern of punishing the *Natur* aspect of humanity in order to lead it to the promised land, or rather a higher plane of being. But the result is aimlessness, signified by the motif of fog. The consequence, on a cultural level, could be the herd mentality symbolized by the people, a mentality which ironically had no greater enemy than Wagner. The presence of the two composers points out that the hostility towards (human) nature was a common pattern of thought among leading cultural figures from the nineteenth century, the century with which Haller identifies.

Similarly, the car hunt concerns achieving a higher state of being, but it also represents a conflict about the means of attaining that goal. The one side in the senseless war against the machine believes that humanity's salvation lies in destroying industrial society. Once the world is rid of oppressive cultural shackles, the way is clear to return to nature. This side calls on people to take the side of the humans by attacking the ruthless rich. But they do not stop there: they hope to destroy industrial civilization so that nature may once again flourish. In a sense, the pro-nature faction is motivated by the desire to escape the guilt stemming from the loss of paradise by returning to a naive harmony with nature. In other words, they seek a kind of promised land, which the figures of Brahms and Wagner appear to be seeking in the Magic Theater. To achieve their ends, the pro-nature faction would have to destroy not just modern society, but civilization per se.

The other side fights for civilization. It extols the blessing of order, work, property and culture. The machine, this side argues, is the highest invention of the human spirit and will transform individuals into gods, or immortals, to use Haller's term. In effect, both sides believe that humanity can attain completeness, but in reality neither side can reach its goal. There can be no utopia with the machine if society destroys nature and the value of the individual. Likewise, there can be no return to nature: returning to nature by using industrially produced weapons is an oxymoron.

That the pacifist Haller takes part in the violent anarchy reveals his aggression. In part, his aggression stems from his self-hatred, which is caused by his separation from the immortals. After his visit with Mozart, Haller appears almost determined to reverse violently the process by which he gains a high level of self-understanding in the Magic Theater. As he stands alone in the hallway, he smashes a mirror in which he sees one of his own images; this destructive act represents an attempt to stop the process of self-reflection. Haller then reaches into his pocket to find the game figures. Instead, he pulls out a knife, as if the pieces of his personality have merged into a tool for carrying out aggressive impulses. In fact, he uses the knife to kill Hermine when he finds her lying naked next to Pablo.

The meaning of the murder has never been conclusively resolved in the secondary literature. While nearly all argue that Haller is called upon to achieve psychic wholeness, there is no consensus on whether the stabbing of Hermine represents progress to that end. Mileck believes that the murder of Hermine is a necessary step to attaining wholeness (192), a view that is disputed by others (Timms 179, Völker 50). The same two positions mark the terrain among psychoanalytic critics. Hans Lüthi[21] and Mark Boulby[22] argue that the killing of Hermine represents the attack of Logos on the anima. But one Jungian scholar argues that "...having assimilated the anima projection by killing Hermine, Harry Haller is 'condemned' to continue living" (Maier 154). Another Jungian scholar interprets the Minotaur myth as follows: Theseus' rescue of Ariadne "...(s)ymbolizes the liberation of the anima figure from the devouring mother image."[23] But Hermine is in no way a "devouring mother" to Haller. At the ball, she functions as the eternal feminine. In Jungian terms, the eternal feminine is the mediator between the conscious ego and the unconscious (von Franz 196). I share the views of Lüthi, Boulby, and von Franz, but I would like to examine the importance of Pablo in a Jungian context as well. Pablo, as the shadow, represents repressed aspects of Haller's psyche. According to the treatise, the union of Pablo and Hermine represents the union of the "Urvater" of spirit and the "Urmutter" of nature. In Jungian theory, it would represent the union of the anima and the shadow of Haller's psyche. Indeed, Haller needs the elements of his personality which Hermine represents. This explains why the Pablo-Mozart figure eventually gives Haller a Hermine game figurine to keep. Moreover, Hermine is identified with nature and eros, the very forces which enable Haller to enjoy a second development in "Alle Mädchen sind dein" in much the same fashion as the treatise delineates.

In short, Haller's aggressive actions thwart him from achieving wholeness, and by extension, immortality. In Jungian terms, Haller has not yet integrated the female or nature element into his personality and he should learn from Pablo, who loves women and men. The Pablo-Mozart figure also unifies the spirit-sensuality on a higher plane, that of the artist who observes life from a critical distance. Thus, he is a *Vor-bild*, both an example and an image of wholeness to which Haller aspires. The connection to Dionysus shows that composing a personality requires reflection and an enthusiastic affirmation of life. Thus, Haller would have done better to join Hermine and Pablo.

Haller's shabby justification of his crime indicates that he has not conquered his dread; he is still fearful of individuation and love. Haller proclaims his guilt to Mozart, and is fully prepared to be executed. Mozart's appearance may well be a sign of how close Haller is to becoming truly immortal. Mozart-Pablo, on the other hand, condemns Haller to continue leading his mortal existence in the real world. Only then will he be permitted to come back to the Magic Theater. Haller will have to find the golden path to the immortals in the slime of the world.

4.10 Summary

The motif of the labyrinth in Hesse's *Steppenwolf* is a signifier of the crisis of European culture at the beginning of the early twentieth century. The desolate, lifeless city captures the petrification of bourgeois culture that shaped intellectual life in Germany in the nineteenth century. The motif of the labyrinth in *Der Steppenwolf* has the same constituent elements as its counterpart in Kafka's *Prozeß*: the motifs of the path, light, darkness, and the house.

The fact that Haller comes far closer to finding the meaning of life than K. can be attributed to the different conception of the two figures. In contrast to K., Haller has an intellectual orientation in life and proves to be capable of learning. Haller is a reflective writer who identifies with the Classical-Romantic tradition and is well-versed in contemporary politics. Haller is an allegory of German *Geist*; his orientation in the city labyrinth is a cipher for the direction of *Geist* in modern society. Although he frequently criticizes contemporary culture, Haller's personal crisis actually mirrors the cultural crisis. His existential dilemma is caused by the tension between spirit and nature. In more concrete terms, the figure cannot intellectually confront his own existence as an embodied, mortal subject. This intellectual confusion is signified by the motif of darkness, which appears in conjunction with dread and aggression. This configuration occurs in Kafka's *Prozeß* as well; the success of the questers' movements through the labyrinth hinges on their developing a new relationship to the body. The motif of eros, however, has significantly different functions in the two texts. There is in *Der Prozeß* a dialectically structured (intellectual vs. material) discourse of the body. Erotic desire is a symptom of a material relationship to corporality and precludes any intellectual reflection on life. In Hesse's *Steppenwolf*, eros unifies polarities; sensuous experiences bring Haller, the representative of *Geist*, in touch with his own long repressed *Natur*. In fact, eros propels Haller onto the path to light at the ball, whereas K.'s erotic desire frequently leads him onto the path to darkness.

The representation of Haller's psyche as the Magic Theater labyrinth is a technique which seems to be a deliberate application of Jungian psychology. The Magic Theater establishes yet another parallel between *Der Steppenwolf* and *Der Prozeß*. In both texts, there is a city labyrinth as well as a second labyrinth, the Magic Theater and the hermeneutical labyrinth respectively, which captures the challenging nature of self- and cultural reflection. Both are intellectual labyrinths which demarcate the individual's possibility of attaining self-realization by developing an ethical interpretation of life in the world. Haller can quite literally transcend his mortal, empirical being: he can become immortal by understanding the (sensuous) life experiences behind the Classical-Romantic cultural codes. This kind of intellectual growth presupposes an interpreter who already knows the cultural codes and who can gain a new understanding of life by having new experiences of his own embodiment. In Kafka's *Prozeß* it is nearly impossible to find the way out of the cultural crisis because modern individuals do not understand social or cultural forces.

CHAPTER 5

Labyrinths of Decadence in Mann's *Zauberberg*

5.1 Introduction

The motif of the labyrinth in *Der Prozeß* and *Der Steppenwolf* signifies intellectual disorientation. In Hesse's *Steppenwolf*, the labyrinth of the Magic Theater is a cipher for the difficulty of reflecting on the relation between self and world, and in this respect, it functions much like the motif of the labyrinth in Mann's *Zauberberg*. The sheer number of doors underscores the challenging nature of reflection in the Magic Theater, but it is critical not to lose sight of the purpose of reflection: the protagonists gain the insight necessary to leading a meaningful existence in the real world. The Pablo-Mozart figure admonishes Haller to come to terms with the flawed nature of the world and to accept the burden of living.

There are striking similarities between Hesse's *Steppenwolf* and Thomas Mann's *Tod in Venedig*[1] and *Zauberberg*. Both Haller and Gustav von Aschenbach are writers. Aschenbach and Haller alike stand in the nineteenth century literary tradition, and both strive to guide the intellectual life of their readers through their works. It is in this context that form plays a significant role in Aschenbach's works. For Aschenbach, giving artistic form to his works is a matter of giving ethical form:

> ...sein Stil entriet in späteren Jahren der unmittelbaren Kühnheiten, der subtilen und neuen Abschattungen, er wandelte sich ins Mustergültig-Feststehende, Geschliffen-Herkömmliche, Erhaltende, Formelle, selbst Formelhafte.... (Mann, *GW* 8: 456)

In Mann's own thinking, form exemplifies the Apollonian principle of order. At the same time, the quote suggests that the emphasis on form is making Aschenbach's texts grow stale. His eventual fate reveals that he rigidly maintains form by suppressing the sensuous, an unambiguous sign that cracks are appearing in the foundation of idealist aesthetics.

Aschenbach, like Haller, is a writer who enters a city labyrinth. Venice is "das trübe Labyrinth der Kanäle" (Mann, *GW* 8: 480). Further, Aschenbach's decisive movements into and within the labyrinth are inspired by dreams and visions. In the beginning, Aschenbach is enticed by a dream of exotic lands in the East, but eventually decides to go to Venice instead, where he falls in love with the Polish boy Tadzio. Aschenbach's passion compels him to stay in Venice, a city of seductive beauty and disease. The disease is not only an affliction of the body but also a cipher for moral decay, the surrender to destructive elemental forces. Specifically, Aschenbach falls victim to the bodily drives of eros and thanatos. The triumph of these Dionysian forces over the Apollonian is objectified in his dream of a group of frenzied dancers celebrating a kind of mythic ritual. Aschenbach's subsequent death represents a plunge into the abyss of formlessness. The Venice labyrinth, then, is joined in a signifying nexus with sensuality, disease (the dissolution of moral form), and death. In other words, Aschenbach's demise effectively contravenes the tenets of idealist aesthetics as Eagleton defines it. In both Mann's *Tod in Venedig* and Hesse's *Steppenwolf*, dreams and visions are linked to the sensuous, bodily realm and at the same time represent a kind of descent into the murky depths of the unconscious. Additionally, the dreams have far-reaching implications for renewing bourgeois culture, which was showing more and more signs of ossification in the early twentieth century. In *Der Steppenwolf*, this movement into the unconscious is a necessary step in establishing new and more meaningful values, whereas *Der Tod in Venedig* shows that this plunge can lead to barbarism if thanatos is not held in check.

The comparison with *Der Tod in Venedig* and *Der Steppenwolf* illuminates central aspects of the motif of the labyrinth in *Der Zauberberg*. In previous research, the sanatorium has not been interpreted as a labyrinth. Helmut Koopmann[2] refers to Berghof as a labyrinth, but does not undertake an examination of the labyrinth and its constituent elements. In *Der Zauberberg*, the Berghof sanatorium, a strange if alluring place which almost seems like an exclusive resort in the mountains of Switzerland, is represented as a labyrinth. The sanatorium labyrinth is a place of reflection in a twofold sense. Life at the sanatorium mirrors cultural currents of Europe, but like the Magic Theater, the sanatorium is not identical to the real world. The strange world at the sanatorium captures the culture of decadence that is thematized in *Der Tod in Venedig*. Although there is no city labyrinth such as Venice in *Der Tod in Venedig*, the sanatorium labyrinth in *Der Zauberberg* does share one essential feature with Venice: it too is a place of decadence, disease, and death. Furthermore, in both texts moral and intellectual decay are signified by disease. In *Der Zauberberg*, the patients continually pursue bodily pleasures and repress any thought of the suffering of the truly ill. Thus, they are not capable of confronting their own mortality. Their inability to come to terms with their corporality is a reflection of the cultural crisis which besets Europe on the eve of the First World War. At the same time, however, the sanatorium can also be a place of reflection in a far different sense. It can be a unique place for reflecting on ontological issues. Castorp learns by studying philosophical, scientific, and historical questions in an attempt to understand the meaning of human existence. Those who seek only pleasure become entrapped in the labyrinth, whereas Castorp, who displays remarkable intellectual growth, traverses the sanatorium labyrinth. In so doing, Castorp finds the meaning of life in terms of corporality. But how he is to take the insights gained in the realm of reflection and, like Haller, apply them in the real world is a vexing question which cannot be answered definitively.

The Berghof sanatorium also shares a number of physical features with the Magic Theater. Like its counterpart in *Der Steppenwolf*, the sanatorium labyrinth has a main path, the hallway, which is intersected by a number of paths marked by doors to the patients' rooms. Castorp is a quester figure who traverses the labyrinth in search of the meaning of life. The key to his quest is corporality in a twofold sense. Like Haller and Josef K., Castorp is challenged to develop an intellectual response to human "Sein zum Tod," to use Heidegger's term. There is an additional aspect to Castorp's quest which is unique to his individuation. Part of Castorp's quest involves studying the body in a variety of discourses including art, science, and philosophy.

The sanatorium labyrinth has two variations: the intellectual labyrinth formed by Castorp's discussions with Behrens, Naphta, and Settembrini about the meaning of life; and the battlefield at the end of the text. Additionally, Castorp's spiralling Crane Dance path on the mountaintop in the chapter "Schnee" is aligned with the motif of the labyrinth. The center of all three labyrinths is the human body. Castorp moves from door to door in traversing the sanatorium labyrinth in the chapter "Totentanz" when he visits the sick as part of his biological study of the body. The central motif cluster path-door-body which occurs in "Totentanz" recurs in Castorp's intellectual labyrinth. He goes to see various conversation partners in whose rooms there are representations of the body. The discussions of these representations give insights into the role of corporality in science, philosophy, and politics. The movement through the intellectual labyrinth is an allegory for the process of reflecting on the function and meaning of the body in different fields. Castorp does not develop his own understanding of life in terms of corporality until he has the dream in the snow. But in the end, Castorp leaves the realm of reflection on the mountain to return to the real world in the throes of a military conflagration. Castorp's decision to fight in the First World War raises troubling questions as to whether he can use his insights to address the cultural crisis which corrodes the intellectual foundation of antebellum Europe. The war is linked to the cultural crisis in *Der Tod in Venedig* and *Der Zauberberg* since the battlefield is represented as a labyrinth. Specific details of the construction of the battlefield landscape essentially mirror details of the Magic Mountain. But the thematic recurrences do not stop there. As I will show, the motifs of love, death, and disease occur on the battlefield as well as on the mountain and in Venice.

Hence, the war in *Der Zauberberg* represents the culmination of the cultural crisis. Since Castorp appears at the end in the war labyrinth, the case can certainly be made that he does not develop an adequate response to the forces which spell doom for Aschenbach in the Venice labyrinth. I would argue that Castorp's movement in the sanatorium labyrinth anticipates essentially the same challenge on a different plane. In this case, his test of orientation in the war labyrinth has cultural and political implications. Castorp's movement on the battlefield must be seen in terms of Mann's changing understanding of the meaning of death and eros in the Romantic tradition.

The pivotal event in the quester's movement through these labyrinths is of course the encounter with death. Mann himself states in *Betrachtungen eines Unpolitischen* that the sympathy with death is an integral element of the Romantic tradition.[3] He in fact states that the sympathy with death expressed in Pfitzner's *Palestrina* corresponds to his own concept of humanity, the notion that each individual is part of a spiritual collective. Castorp is initially afflicted with the sympathy with death (Mann, *GW* 12: 424). In *Der Tod in Venedig*, death is joined in a nexus with disease and eros, a configuration which certainly applies to the patients including Castorp. In the 1920s, however, Mann's concern about the Romantic tradition, above all the misuse of this tradition by political reactionaries, leads to his reevaluation of Romanticism.

Consequently, Mann uses the thinking of Novalis to redefine the relationship of death and eros. This shift is reflected in Castorp's changing relationship to corporality. In "Von deutscher Republik"[4] from 1922, Mann analyzes Novalis's idea of the sympathy with the organic, the erotic attraction to the flesh. It can, according to Mann, be a spiritual experience since "(m)an berührt den Himmel, wenn man einen Menschenleib betastet" (Mann, *GW* 11: 845). In the case of Novalis's "Hymnen an die Nacht," the sympathy with the organic is combined with the sympathy with death, whose symptoms are disease, death, and lust (Mann, *GW* 11: 849). The sympathy with death stems from the desire to reach a higher plane of being, to achieve a spiritual community after death. Its constituent elements are the same ones which are present in the Venice labyrinth. The only way in which these deadly forces can be overcome is if eros is transformed into a kind of caritas, a commitment to a life of serving others. "Keine Metamorphose des Geistes ist uns besser vertraut als die, an deren Anfang die Sympathie mit dem Tode, an deren Ende der Entschluß zum Lebensdienste steht" (Mann, *GW* 11: 851). This points to a critical difference in the function of eros in Hesse's *Steppenwolf* and Mann's *Zauberberg*. Whereas eros in *Der Steppenwolf* is a counterforce to the figure's desire to die, eros in *Der Zauberberg* is aligned with deadly forces. But in both texts, eros can be enhanced so that the figure experiences an expansion in his ability to love. Implicitly, the dangerous attraction to the mysteries of the flesh in *Der Zauberberg* can give the individual a greater understanding of others and of the burdens their embodiment causes.

Mann does not actually state how in Novalis's case the impurities within the Romantic sympathy with death can be cleansed from the sympathy with the organic so that eros can be enhanced. But Mann does find the answer in Goethe's *Wilhelm Meister*. The erotic sphere of the theater first awakens Meister's interest in the human body. This interest is a stepping stone to his study of medicine. From medicine, Meister turns his attention to sociology, politics, and pedagogy, which are all related to medicine by the same object of study: the individual. Mann even suggests that the pattern of development in Goethe's *Wilhelm Meister* is a model for his *Zauberberg*:

> Das Interesse für Tod und Krankheit, für das Pathologische, den Verfall ist nur eine Art von Ausdruck für das Interesse am Leben, am Menschen, wie die humanistische Fakultät der Medizin beweist; wer sich für das Organische, das Leben, interessiert, der interessiert sich namentlich für den Tod; und es könnte Gegenstand eines Bildungsromans sein zu zeigen, daß das Erlebnis des Todes zuletzt ein Erlebnis des Lebens ist, daß es zum *Menschen* führt. (Mann, *GW* 11: 851)

Mann's own readings of Goethe and Novalis provide the matrices for tracking Castorp's development on the mountain and his eventual decision to return to the flatlands. To that end, I will focus on the extent to which the figure of Castorp can be identified either with the healthy sympathy with the organic or the diseased sympathy with death.

5.2 Sanatorium Labyrinth

In contrast to *Der Prozeß* and *Der Steppenwolf*, *Der Zauberberg* has no city per se. Most of the plot unfolds at the Berghof sanatorium situated on a mountain in Switzerland. Consequently, whereas the labyrinth in both *Der Prozeß* and *Der Steppenwolf* was examined in terms of the theme of the city, the sanatorium labyrinth in *Der Zauberberg* must be analyzed with respect to the motif of the mountain. Historically, the mountain can be a place of intense spiritual or sensual experience. In the Western tradition, mountain-top experiences have been associated with clarity of vision, wisdom, and self-insight (Daemmrich 65). In the Hebrew tradition, the mountain was the place of spiritual experiences, and the Greeks believed that Mount Olympus was the home of the Gods. The elevation of the mountain reflects, then, a higher level of knowledge or spirituality. The mountain can also have a different function, which goes back to the Greek tradition, namely, as a place of temptation and seduction. In the Tannhäuser legend, the protagonist experiences sensuous love in a mountain with Venus which results in his condemnation.

Nietzsche locates the origins of Apollonian culture on the Olympian "magic mountain." Apollo is in a sense the father of the Olympian world, the Greek deities who are portrayed in "marvelous shapes" on friezes. Nietzsche asks what the need was for the Olympian and finds the answer in humanity's relationship to nature:

Now it is as if the Olympian magic mountain had opened before us and revealed its roots to us. The Greek knew and felt the terror and horror of existence. That he might endure this terror at all, he had to interpose between himself and life the radiant dream-birth of the Olympians. That overwhelming dismay in the face of the titanic powers of nature...that entire philosophy of the sylvan god, with its mythical exemplars...all this was again and again overcome by the Greeks with the Olympian *middle world* of art.... (Nietzsche, *The Birth of Tragedy* 42)

Both Apollonian and Dionysian cultures attempt to come to terms with the alienation from nature: the Dionysian by seeking a naive return to mystical unity; the Apollonian through their deities. Ultimately, the attitudes stem from existential fear, the awareness of the mortal *Natur* or corporal aspect of humanity. Implicitly the attitude of the Greeks towards nature and corporality is the basis for these two cultural traditions as Nietzsche understands them.

Nietzsche's reading of the Olympian magic mountain adds another dimension to the motif of the mountain. The mountain can be a place where individuals have an intellectual or sensuous experience of human corporality. In Aschenbach's case, sensuous drives are linked to decadence, formlessness, and the Dionysian. Aschenbach perishes in the Venice labyrinth by succumbing to these drives. Likewise, the sanatorium labyrinth in *Der Zauberberg* is a place of wild sensuous pleasures.

The way into the Berghof labyrinth is through sickness. The patients have come for medical reasons or are afflicted by moral disease. In the latter case, they flee from the demands of everyday life in Europe so that they can enjoy a carefree life on the mountain and seek pleasures without any hindrance there. Like Aschenbach, the patients are afflicted with the disease from the East. The former, who falls in love with Tadzio from Eastern Europe, catches Indian cholera whereas the dissolute patients live in a world with a lot of Asia in the air, in the words of Settembrini. The psychiatrist Krokowski sees their physical ailments as caused by repressed (erotic) drives. In a general sense, he is right in that the patients have not come to terms with their own embodiment. But Krokowski's appearance as a figure of death (in his black gown), his dubious practices, and finally, his presence in the labyrinth raise the question of whether he can use science to give intellectual guidance to individuals.

Inside the sanatorium, the layout of the hallways has essentially the same features as the chancelleries in *Der Prozeß* and the Magic Theater in *Der Steppenwolf*. It consists of a main hallway intersected by paths indicated by doors. Since the patients behind the doors are dying, all the paths lead to death. By the same token, the paths also take Castorp to his object of study: the body. It is in fact the human individual which is at the center of the labyrinth. Castorp traverses the labyrinth to find out how his fellow human beings respond to their mortality. When he visits the terminally ill, Castorp makes a series of movements with the identical configuration: path-door-body/death (dying person). The representation of the sanatorium as a labyrinthine underworld is further supported by literary references. The inside of the Berghof even looks like the ancient labyrinths. The walls of the hallway gleam brightly, just like the white polished stone in the labyrinths of Egypt and Crete which Pliny mistakenly identified as Parian marble. Pliny also mentions doors slamming shut in the paths, a sound captured by Mann in continuous references to Clavdia Chauchat's slamming of the hallway door.

Through recurring references to the moon, the representation of the Berghof as a Jericho labyrinth (a sinful city of the moon) is established. According to Settembrini, the smallest unit of time is a month or the length of the cycle of the moon. The main sources of light in the dining hall are the chandeliers. The narrator compares the central light of the chandeliers to the moon. Later, the lighting there is described as a "Lüstermond." In a sense, the dining hall is really illuminated by moonlight.

Literary and mythological references to the mythological underworld establish additional connections to the labyrinthine underworld. Settembrini calls Berghof the "Schattenreich," and doctors Behrens and Krokowski are identified as Rhadamanthus and Minos, respectively, two of the judges of the underworld in Greek mythology. The doctors act as judges since they decide how long patients should stay. Both doctors have their offices downstairs in the basement, and Krokowski's is several steps lower than that of Behrens. Similarly, Minos appears at the second level of Dante's *Inferno* where adulterers are punished in the swirling winds. Along these lines, critics have recently advanced the opinion that Dante's hell is a labyrinth (Gillespie 297, Doob 271-306).

The reference to adultery is fitting because the patients are confined to an underworld of carnal pleasure. In fact, the patients' days revolve around bodily activities. They eat five sumptuous meals a day. At prescribed times they must lie covered on the balcony, which Settembrini calls the "horizontal." This is also the position they take for the other main activity in the rooms, eros. The concupiscence of the patients is symptomatic of their regression to a more primitive, animal-like state of being. As Castorp hears the wild antics of the Russian couple next door, he compares them to animals. Clavdia can also be identified with an animal as is apparent from the last syllable of her surname (*chat*) which means cat in French.

The formlessness of the Berghof world is produced by the lack of intellectual or ethical law to regulate the realm of the body. In point of fact, there is not the slightest hint of intellectual life at the sanatorium. Most of the books in the sanatorium library stand unused on the shelves. The sole book that generates any interest is entitled "Die Kunst zu verführen," a text which offers advice on a topic with which the patients are already well acquainted. Thus, the sanatorium labyrinth captures the intellectual and existential disorientation in the early twentieth century, the same cultural phenomenon about which the city labyrinths in *Der Prozeß* and *Der Steppenwolf* furnish information. Indeed, the patients are at best dimly aware of the cultural tradition. When Joachim dies, Frau Stöhr suggest playing

Beethoven's "Erotika." There can be no clearer example of how the patients' relationship to the body distorts their perception of the cultural tradition.

In addition to the wild sensuality, the heavy eating and drinking of the patients are signs that their way of being is reified (Daemmrich 244). Their material orientation in life is further evidenced by their fear of death; this configuration occurs in Kafka's *Prozeß* as well. While enjoying the seemingly endless repetition of pleasures, they suppress any thought of their own mortality. Frau Stöhr admonishes Castorp for mentioning the death of the Austrian cavalry officer. None of the other patients broaches the subject, and from Joachim's comments, Castorp realizes that death occurs behind the scenes. Their unwillingness to confront death is actually consistent with the references to animals. Castorp senses that Joachim knows that his days are numbered and that his cousin cannot speak about his impending death. For Castorp, Joachims' state of mind illustrates the old adage that as long as we are, death is not, but when death is present, we are not. Since there is no real rapport between death and us, all living beings are able to contemplate death with indifference, irresponsibility and egoistical innocence. Castorp detects a high degree of this irresponsibility and innocence in Joachim's conduct (Mann, *GW* 3: 734).

It is striking that individuals confront death with the innocence of all living creatures, i.e. of animals. It could be then that reification is a sign of wanting to escape the responsibility of living. These patterns show that the individual must face death in order to understand life. The reference to animals is a sign that the patients are intellectually unable to confront the process of human individuation which according to Schopenhauer is a result of corporality. The patients share a characteristic with Josef K. in Kafka's *Prozeß*. Their material relationship to the flesh leaves them trapped in a labyrinth of formlessness and death.

5.3 Castorp: Quester Figure

Given Castorp's family background, he is a rather unlikely quester figure to tackle some of the most complex issues in Western culture. He is a member of an elite patrician family in Hamburg. At the beginning of the text, he is described as an unassuming engineer who much prefers comfort and leisure to the demands and rigors of work. He is at best a mediocre student; he only decides to study so that he could eventually sustain his standard of living. In short, Castorp does not in any way distinguish himself in his youth. In part, his disinclination to work is a sign of the times, as the narrator points out. Castorp lives in an age in which there is no real purpose in work. This is a kind of societal disease which first lames the moral self and eventually afflicts the bodies of individuals (Mann, *GW* 3: 50).

The reference to disease clearly indicates that Europe, or the "flatlands," is in the process of decay that takes on such striking forms on the mountain. Castorp's personality development is then in no small part shaped by unhealthy cultural forces in his environment. The expansion of the patterns signifying the moral decay of Europe will expand during Castorp's stay on the mountain through references to music.

In addition to environmental factors, heredity plays a powerful role in Castorp's development. Heredity must be considered in light of Mann's notion of humanity. Mann defines the inward-directed process of personality development in terms of humanity: "Versenkung, ein individualistisches Kulturgewissen; der auf Pflege, Formung, Vertiefung und Vollendung des eigenen Ichs...gerichtete Sinn...."[5] The core of the "Ich" is a common spirit which joins individuals in an intellectual community: "...die Idee der Gemeinschaft bei Anerkennung der Menschheit in jedem ihrer Einzelglieder, die Idee der Humanität, die wir innerlich menschlich und staatlich, aristokratisch und sozial nannten... (Mann, *GW* 11: 835). As Berman shows, humanity remains the basis of Mann's thinking on cultural and political relations in the 1920s (268). The idea that all individuals are spiritual kin has far-reaching implications for the individual's relationship to the community. The individual should engage others on the basis of respect, tolerance, and above all human love since they face the same difficulties in life. As an example of humanity, Mann cites Goethe's *Iphigenie*.[6]

The idea of the body is implicit in the concept of humanity. The individual is a manifestation of a common spirit. This corresponds to Schopenhauer's principium individuum according to which the body of the individual is a product of the common will. Mann himself makes this point in his essay "Schopenhauer"[7] from 1938. In this context, it is little wonder that Castorp studies the body in a variety of different fields to understand the meaning of life.

On the basis of Mann's concept of humanity, figures from the same family in some of literary texts are products of a common entelechy. Thomas Buddenbrook, for example, is comforted by the thought that the spirit of which he is a part will live on in his son Hanno after he dies. Likewise, Hans Castorp is a manifestation of a common Castorp entelechy that defines his position in a generational chain of being. Castorp actually senses this himself as a child when his grandfather shows him the family baptismal bowl. Engraved on the bowl are the names of its owners, Castorp's paternal ancestors. Seeing his grandfather bent over the bowl, just as he was seventy-five years earlier at his own baptism, gives young Castorp the sense of continuity over generations.

The idea of generational continuity in the works of Thomas Mann has received substantial attention in secondary literature. Erich Heller[8] notes that the question "how to equip the typical with individuality, how to win freedom for that which is fated, and how to give meaning and direction to a life running its course in cyclic repetitiveness" is a persistent issue for Mann (E. Heller 194). Manfred Dierks[9] believes that young Castorp has a similar experience to Schopenhauer's *nunc stans* in looking at the bowl; "...die Vorväter, von denen die Taufschale berichtet, rücken dem Knaben zur überindividuellen Gattung (*species*) zusammen..." (Dierks 56). Castorp then stands in a typological relationship to his ancestors. He is not so much an individual as another manifestation of the long tradition of Castorps.[10]

As his grandfather presents the bowl, he pronounces the names of its previous owners; the "ur-ur" sound gives Castorp a spiritual sensation. Castorp identifies with the qualities such as tradition, piety, and conservatism which his grandfather personifies. Castorp's reaction to the baptismal bowl also reveals his fascination with death. Hearing his grandfather pronounce the names of its owners gives young Castorp the feeling of breathing the damp air from the Catharine church or the Michaelis crypt. Castorp's sensations correspond exactly to Mann's conceptual triad "Kreuz, Gruft und Tod," his shorthand formulation for the German cultural tradition in the nineteenth century in *Betrachtungen eines Unpolitischen*. Thus, Castorp can be seen as a representative of his family and the German cultural tradition as well. Castorp's intellectual orientation can be seen as an allegory for the cultural orientation of Germany. After all, a figure from Western Europe (Settembrini) and Eastern Europe (Clavdia) identify Castorp as a representative of Germany. As Castorp is presented with conflicting ideas, philosophies and attitudes towards life from representatives from the West (Settembrini) and the East (Clavdia and Naphta), he faces essentially the same intellectual challenges with which, in Mann's view, Germany is confronted. In short, the figure of Castorp is situated on the same levels of signification as Haller is in Hesse's *Steppenwolf*.

5.4 Ascent up the Mountain: The Wooded Grove

Castorp's search for the meaning of life ultimately leads him from the sanatorium to the mountain range. His movement is identified by the patterns fog/haze-light. When Castorp walks to the grove in the chapter "Hippe," clouds cover the sky. In the chapter "Schnee," there are again clouds. In addition, the falling snow creates a dense haze which blankets Davos and the mountain top. Ultimately, Castorp must take this path out of the sanatorium labyrinth in order to find the meaning of life.

Clouds are in the sky when Castorp first moves up the mountain. In the chapter "Hippe," he goes for a walk up the mountain and stops at a wooded grove. The landscape at the grove has strong allusions to Romanticism. Castorp stops in the woods near a rushing stream, a common topos in Romantic poetry. Castorp also enjoys listening to the stream with the same sleepy pious expression he has when he listens to music and when his grandfather pronounce the names of his ancestors. The ground is covered with blue flowers. The blue flower was an important motif in German Romanticism in general, and for Novalis in particular. In *Heinrich von Ofterdingen* by Novalis, Heinrich sees the face of a young girl in a blue flower in the dream. The blue flower has, according to Géza von Molnár[11] a mediating function in the quest to fuse polarities into a higher unity. The central poles, self-world, were to be joined by eros (von Molnár 115). In Novalis's thinking, the spirit of poesy, a creative principle, should redefine the relationship between self and world from the perspective of freedom (von Molnár 118). At the end of Heinrich's quest, the dichotomy between self and world collapses, whereby the world becomes dream (the inner world of the self) and dream becomes world (von Molnár 124).

By dreaming, he enters a state of mind which corresponds to the Romantic ideal of freeing consciousness from the causality of the outer world. The narrator states that his self moves to a distant time and space. Castorp dreams of Hippe, an old school mate who first aroused erotic feelings in him. He realizes that it is Hippe who reminds him of Clavdia; in fact, they have the same grayish blue eyes. Clavdia then is the reappearance of the Slavic figure at a higher level. The object of Castorp's quest is the Slavic figure, which indicates to us Castorp's longing for wholeness. The reader can see that Hippe is also a figure of eros and thanatos. Hippe is the object of Castorp's desire and his name means the scythe of Death in Middle German (*Deutsches Wörterbuch*[1] IV, 2; 1552). It is important to note that love, as eros, is the complement of death. The relationship between love and death will change

change markedly in the chapter "Schnee." At this juncture, however, Castorp is afflicted with a form of the insidious sympathy with death which Mann identifies with Novalis's "Brautbett" poetry. These latent forces in Castorp appear as disease.

The similarity between Castorp and Aschenbach (in *Der Tod in Venedig*) points to the dangers implicit in Castorp's dream. Both figures have homoerotic feelings for a figure from the East. In "Pariser Rechenschaft,"[12] Mann connects the Dionysian, to which Aschenbach falls victim, to both the East and Romanticism. When Aschenbach succumbs to Dionysian forces, he falls into an abyss of formlessness. Hence, by extension, Castorp's Romantic desire for self-transcendence through death can ultimately lead to self-dissolution. For Castorp, the dissolution of the material appears to be the means to attain a higher unity of being.

To be sure, eros and death are also linked to the patients. If Castorp is to find the meaning of life, he must be exposed to the forces of decay which threaten life. This suggests further that the quester figure can only find a response to the disease afflicting European civilization by first contracting the disease.

5.5 Light-Dark(Clouds)

When Castorp moves to the wooded grove, the motif of fog (clouds), a supporting motif of the labyrinth, occurs and gives information on Castorp's sympathy with death. In Castorp's conversation with Settembrini in the chapter "Kahnfahrt," the motif pattern is expanded to encompass light and dark (fog). In his mind, Castorp associates the two grandfathers first with the sky and then with larger historical traditions. Further, the body links these constituent elements of the labyrinth with the Enlightenment and Romanticism.

One evening after dinner, Settembrini tells the cousins about his revolutionary grandfather Giuseppe. The conservative Castorp is taken aback by Giuseppe Settembrini's politics. Nevertheless, Joachim and Castorp realize that Giuseppe's politics does not make him any less patriotic than they are. On the contrary, the revolutionary Giuseppe was a republican patriot. Castorp compares Giuseppe Settembrini, a representative of the progressive tradition in the West, with his own grandfather, a representative of the conservative tradition in Germany. As Castorp visualizes the two grandfathers in his mind, they become the embodiment of the respective traditions. He imagines Giuseppe Settembrini leading a group of freedom fighters, his own grandfather with his head bent over the baptismal bowl as his lips form the "Ur-Ur" sound. As different as the two grandfathers were, they both adorned their bodies in black gowns to mourn the state of the present:

> Aber der eine hatte es aus Frömmigkeit getan, der Vergangenheit und dem Tode zu Ehren, denen sein Wesen angehörte; der andere dagegen aus Rebellion und zu Ehren eines frömmigkeitsfeindlichen Fortschritts. (Mann, *GW* 3: 217)

Castorp first connects the grandfathers to cultural traditions. They represent two worlds, he thinks, or more precisely, two regions of the sky. Castorp associates Giuseppe Settembrini with the Western sky where there was a clear, bright, sunny day; and his own grandfather with the Eastern sky where there was a dark, foggy, moonlit night. The sunshine in the West is a metaphor for the Enlightenment, whereas the fog in the East is a metaphor for German Romanticism. In the Enlightenment, the motif of light can signify the effort to establish a world order based on reason (Daemmrich 214), which was certainly the hope of Giuseppe Settembrini. The light in the West stands for reason, a faculty of the mind which Mann frequently and vociferously attacks in *Betrachtungen eines Unpolitischen*. In the Enlightenment and Classicism, the motif of the night signifies thinking that is opposed to the Enlightenment. This idea is supported by the motif of fog which serves to block the light. In Romanticism, it could ease the transition from conscious thinking to fantasy and intensify emotional experiences (Daemmrich 235). Thus, for Castorp, the grandfathers serve to link intellectual currents with this scene in physical space.

Mann of course identifies himself with the German Romantic tradition. In discussing the Romanticism of Pfitzner's *Palestrina*, Mann draws a distinction between the Enlightenment and Romanticism which echoes Castorp's comparison of the grandfathers:

> Wirklich ist der "Palestrina" eine Dichtung, die obwohl ethisch noch höher stehend, als künstlerisch, des fortschrittlichen Optimismus, der politischen *Tugend* also, völlig entbehrt. Sie ist Romantik...ihre Sympathie gilt nicht dem Neuen, sondern dem Alten, nicht der Zukunft, sondern der Vergangenheit, nicht dem Leben, sondern-... (Mann, *GW* 12: 413)

Later, Mann adds the missing phrase after the dash: the sympathy with death, which, in *Betrachtungen eines Unpolitischen*, he defines as the core of Romanticism.

The contrasting motif pattern of the sky is expanded as Settembrini continues to explain the political activity of his family. For their part, the Settembrinis have fought for reason, the republic, and the beautiful style in writing. He lauds an important ally in the struggle, Carducci, who attacked Christian sentimental literature and Romanticism, especially the "...Schatten- und Mondscheinpoesie des Romanticismo, den er der...'bleichen Himmelsnonne Luna' verglichen habe!" (Mann, *GW* 3: 226).

While Settembrini presses on in his attack of the East, Castorp seems to listen outwardly while his soul resists inwardly. When he mentally deserts Settembrini in favor of Clavdia, it is as if he is again in the boat paddling from the West to the foggy East. By associating Clavdia with the Eastern sky, the figure of Castorp enlarges the field of signification of the motif of fog. Previously, he identified the dark, foggy sky with his grandfather's piety and longing to return to the past. Now the reference to Clavdia, a recurrence of the Hippe figure, links the sky to death and eros, the two elements that define Castorp's relationship to corporality. Eros must not be understood as the opposite of piety and history, but, in the Romantic context, their complement.

In "Pariser Rechenschaft," Mann asserts that the interest of the Heidelberg Romantics in death, nature, and the past has erotic roots. The thinking of the Heidelberg Romantics is according to Mann "...bestimmt von dem großen 'Zurück' von der mütterlich-nächtigen Idee der Vergangenheit" (Mann, *GW* 11: 48-49). Implicitly, the term "mütterlich" equates the return to the past with a return to the womb. Mann actually suggests this when he terms the Romantic nationalist nostalgia a "Zurück in den mystisch-historisch-romantischen Mutterschoß" (Mann, *GW* 11: 50). Hence, the light is associated with a form of thinking which envisions a more perfect world in the future based on reason and virtue, or *Tugend*, the word Mann uses in the quote about Pfitzner. The fog, on the other hand, stands for a type of thinking which envisions a reconstruction of a past world on the basis of spiritual forces in nature and, by extension, human *Natur*—the body. The motifs relating to corporality connect the contrasting skies in Castorp's vision with the German cultural tradition. This is congruent with Nietzsche's reading of the Apollonian and the Dionysian. The motif patterns indicate further that Castorp's search for the meaning of life in terms of the body must include reflection on the German cultural tradition, a tradition which is in part shaped by attitudes towards the body. A crucial step in Castorp's personal and intellectual development is study of how individuals confront their mortal, empirical being.

5.6 Movement through the Labyrinth: Path-Door-Body

When Castorp moves through the sanatorium labyrinth, the configuration path-door-body occurs. Castorp makes a series of visits with dying patients in the chapter "Totentanz." By entering their rooms, he goes through the doorway to observe how they confront death. Hence, in contrast to Josef K. in the chancellery, Castorp does not shrink back from the encounter with death. Rather, he gains knowledge into how people confront mortality.

In a sense, Castorp's visits are the logical result of his biological studies in the preceding chapter, "Forschungen." In his determination to find out what life is, Castorp devours books on biology and the human body. His studies mark an important step in his intellectual development. Castorp's efforts are far more demanding than the activities of the patients who indulge in such mindless pursuits as watching the stereoscope. Moreover, Castorp is learning on his own, not only by listening to the advice of Settembrini. Castorp, like Wilhelm Meister, studies organic material, the basis of human corporality. This represents a kind of self-reflection for "Bewußtsein seiner selbst war also schlechthin eine Funktion der zum Leben geordneten Materie, und bei höherer Verstärkung wandte die Funktion sich gegen ihren eigenen Träger..." (Mann, GW 3: 383). For Castorp, reflection on life is rooted in the attraction to the flesh; at the end of his readings, he has a vision of an alluring "Bild des Lebens." For Castorp and Meister alike, the scientific interest in the body is fueled by eros, a component of the sympathy with the organic.[13]

The fact there are two facets of Castorp's desire, love and learning, is especially significant, since in Castorp's case, the sympathy with the organic is linked to the sympathy with death. Castorp's intellectual desire prevents him from succumbing to the menace of death and disease in the labyrinth, the same forces to which Aschenbach falls victim. In other words, Castorp's curiosity about the meaning of life keeps the sympathy with death in check as he traverses the sanatorium. To be sure, Castorp also visits the dying because he himself is fascinated with death. When he enters their rooms, he assumes the same sleepy, pious pose that he strikes when viewing his grandfather's corpse. Castorp is clearly having a spiritual experience of death which is symptomatic of his sympathy with death. But at the same time, an additional reason that Castorp visits the dying is his desire to learn how individuals face their *Sein zum Tod*. Further, he is genuinely concerned about the terminally ill, the forgotten and neglected people at the Berghof. His care is a form of caritas, human love for others based on the recognition that the human individual must bear a heavy burden of suffering in life. In "Goethe und Tolstoi" Mann defines love along these lines:

> Beruht nicht alle *Liebe* zum Menschen auf der sympathievollen, brüderlich-mitbeteiligten Erkenntnis dieser seiner fast hoffnungslos schwierigen Situation? Ja, es gibt einen Menschheitspatriotismus auf dieser Basis: man liebt den Menschen, weil er es schwer hat- und weil man selbst einer ist. (Mann, *GW* 9: 81)

In short, love and the desire to learn recur in varied form as Castorp goes from door to door. The main lesson of his movement through the labyrinth is that most individuals cannot confront their mortality because of their fear of death. They never mention death, and some dying women even enjoy flirting with the two "cavaliers"; hence, the configuration eros-sickness-death recurs in conjunction with the terminally ill patients. Mann's purely negative definition of disease in "Goethe und Tolstoi" applies to the dying:

> Krankheit hat...eine doppelte Beziehung zum Menschlichen und seiner Würde. Sie ist einerseits dieser Würde feindlich, indem sie durch Überbetonung des Körperlichen, durch ein Zurückweisen und Zurückwerfen des Menschen auf seinen Körper herabwürdigt. Andererseits aber ist es möglich, Krankheit sogar als etwas höchst Menschen-würdiges zu denken...Denn wenn es zu weit ginge zu sagen, daß Krankheit Geist, oder...daß Geist Krankheit sei, so haben diese Begriffe doch viel miteinander zu tun. (Mann, *GW* 9: 79-80)

To put it in simpler terms, disease can reduce the individual to a body without mind (*Geist*), or it can alternatively represent an intellectual enhancement in the individual.

The next route which Castorp explores on his movement through the labyrinth is the path to Clavdia's bedroom. Unlike the other patients, she is not terminally ill, and Castorp does not come to console her but to sleep with her in the chapter "Walpurgisnacht." Nevertheless, this episode must be considered in context with Castorp's care for the dying because Castorp's fascination with decaying organic material extends to his relationship with Clavdia as well. His encounter with her continues his experiments with corporality; he even explains his love for her in terms of the body. Love and death, he asserts, are corporal and this is the reason for the terror they cause and their magical effect. Eros and death are of course the constituent elements of the sympathy with death, the same force which manifests itself as disease in Castorp when he has his dream of the Hippe-Clavdia figure in the grove. Hence, the motif pattern eros-sickness-death which appeared in conjunction with the patients, applies in varied form to him.

I suggest that it is his desire to grow intellectually from this experience that saves him. Castorp keeps an x-ray of Clavdia as a souvenir from their liaison. While this is a truly bizarre memento from a tryst, the x-ray is an appropriate item for someone who conducts scientific studies of bodily structures. Thus, it is a strange reminder of the object of erotic desire, but is well-suited for his intellectual desire. Further, on "Walpurgisnacht," Clavdia is identified with Circe, who in Greek mythology turns men into pigs. But there is no sign that Castorp's passion has reduced him to a mere animal, *Natur* without *Geist*, like his wild Russian neighbors. On the contrary, Castorp returns to his intellectual pursuits with renewed interest. He studies astronomy and comes to the conclusion that time is cyclical. Castorp's finding could well stem from his knowledge of biology, for he has already learned that "...der vielzellige Organismus war nur eine Erscheinungsform des zyklischen Prozesses, in dem das Leben sich abspielte, und der ein Kreislauf von Zeugung zu Zeugung war" (Mann, *GW* 3: 388). Thus, Castorp's continued and growing willingness to learn, which has erotic roots, saves him from Aschenbach's fate. Castorp's research and intellectual development also prepare him for his movement through the intellectual labyrinth.

5.7 Intellectual Labyrinth

In contrast to the other patients, Castorp is intellectually curious. Whereas they know only one kind of desire, the desire for the flesh, Castorp also strives to understand life with respect to the body. He therefore seeks out conversation partners who explain their views on human existence. Castorp's pattern of movement represents a variation of his movement through the sanatorium labyrinth, a movement which is supported by the motif cluster path-door-body. Similarly, Castorp goes down a series of paths to visit Dr. Behrens, Naphta, and Settembrini. He crosses through the doorway to their apartments; inside, a representation of the body (the portrait of Clavdia in Behrens' room and the pietà in Naphta's apartment) serves as a basis of discussion. The dialogues about the images of the body show how corporality has shaped scientific, political, and philosophical discourses about human life. These discourses of the body together form an intellectual labyrinth. Castorp's movement to his conversation partners is an allegory for his movement through an intellectual labyrinth on corporality.

Castorp first goes to see Behrens who had actually painted the portrait of Clavdia. The portrait is a stark contrast to the images of the body Behrens scrutinizes in the laboratory. As a doctor, Behrens is used to seeing x-rays of the patients in which the human body is reduced to two dimensional images in black and white. On these images Behrens can look inside the human body. As a painter he cannot accurately reproduce the unique outer appearance of an individual. His portrait of Clavdia is badly distorted and does not in the least do justice to her physiognomy.

Behrens tells Castorp that his subcutaneous knowledge of bodily tissues aids him in painting portraits. But he fails to capture the realistic semblance of an individual or the essential features of the human form. His reference to tissues becomes part of a longer discussion of the structure of organic material. In the conversation, he talks as a scientist who gives priority to the formal over the material. He states that life consists of the preservation of form through the change of substance. Although Behrens describes life in terms of processes, he cannot give meaning to the life process. When he later consoles Joachim's mother, he notes that we are ignorant of birth and death because we do not experience them, i.e. they are devoid of subjective character.

By implication, he can describe no object of analysis which lacks subjective character. If life is form between two mysteries, then understanding life necessitates experiencing the subjective character of form. Indeed, in spite of his scientific knowledge of the body, his portrait of Clavdia bespeaks a subjective, if not emotional, relationship to the flesh. Behrens' painting of Clavdia may well stem from his romantic interest in her because the portrait is painted with "feeling." This points to an attraction to a female Venus figure associated with death and eros.

The objects in the apartment point to unresolved contradictions in Behrens' view of life. He, too, is under the spell of sympathy with the organic, as there are a number of signs of death and eros. The doctor has "...ein Rauchkabinett, das "türkisch" eingerichtet war" (Mann, *GW* 3: 356). Behrens has stayed on the mountain because of his deceased wife or, in other words, because he is bound to her grave (Mann, *GW* 3: 209). A more recent romantic interest, the Egyptian princess, has given him a coffee mill with scenes that are so erotic that the doctor does not let his maid see it. With regard to the labyrinth, the princess is a latter day Isis, a goddess who in some versions of the myth saved her brother's penis. Similarly, the coffee mill is tubular, and the strong coffee seems to have an aphrodisiac quality. The decor of the "Rauchkabinett," the origin of the coffee mill and the portrait of Clavdia all allude to the East, the realm of sensuous pleasure. Thus, Behrens who explains life in formal terms, is himself tied to the sanatorium, the realm of disease and formlessness. That Behrens is afflicted with the disease casts doubt on whether he can objectively use scientific knowledge of the body to improve the life of the community of the patients.

Conversely, the conversation about the pietà leads to a debate on how a more perfect community can be realized. The debate, in which the contrasting views of Naphta and Settembrini are presented, begins with a discussion on the depiction of the body in Naphta's apartment. In the thinking of Naphta and Settembrini alike, the artistic depiction of the body has a representative function. Their ideas are inseparable from their respective positions on the *Natur-Geist* duality of humanity. Whereas Behrens' portrait of Clavdia is supposed to be a realistic portrayal of an individual, the figures in the pietà are deliberately distorted, but for different reasons. Naphta lauds the pietà. In his opinion, it reminds the viewer of the conflict between sensuality and spirituality, or in other words, between the human body and the divine spirit; more precisely, the pietà deals with the emancipation of the spirit from the natural. Further, Naphta argues, the pietà signifies the suffering inherent in the human condition brought about by the weakness of the flesh. According to the Jesuit Naphta, the beauty of the body is abstract, the only true beauty is the beauty of religious expression.

Settembrini counters that the pietà represents the degradation of human dignity. In art, the body should show the beauty of the human form. The viewer should see a representation of the human spirit in harmony with nature. He explains his ideal as that of the classical heritage: form, beauty, reason, and the pagan joy of life. Essentially, Settembrini and Naphta define the body as either the battleground between spirit and nature or the place where they are harmoniously joined. Naphta who stands in the tradition of scholasticism explains how their philosophical standpoints can be traced back to opposing scientific doctrines.

If Ptolemy is right, Naphta explains, the world is finite in time and space. The deity is then transcendent, the antithesis between God and humanity remains unresolved, and human existence is dual. The problem of the human soul consists of the conflict between the spiritual and the material. All social problems are secondary to this conflict. If, on the other hand, Renaissance astronomers are right, then the cosmos is infinite. In that case, Settembrini can correctly argue that there is no suprasensible world and no dualism. The antithesis between God and nature disappears and the human personality ceases to be the theater of battle between two hostile principles. The only real problem left, Naphta concludes, is the conflict between individual and collective interests (Mann, *GW* 3: 552-553).

Naphta's exegesis reveals that their political philosophies are based on different scientific conceptions of the spirit-nature polarity. To be sure, their attitudes towards the body are not explicitly articulated in Naphta's statement. Nevertheless, the positions of Naphta and Settembrini on the spiritual/intellectual versus the sensuous/empirical aspects of being are the basis for their understanding of the human individual as well as of their understanding of the relationship of the individual to the community. In this context, it is fair to say that the political ideologies of the two intellectuals are shaped by their respective attitudes towards corporality. Clearly, Naphta believes that human sensuality (nature) should be combatted. He advocates a mystical, authoritarian, socialistic community to achieve the spiritual salvation of each individual soul. In his ideal state, all available means are used to prevent individuals from succumbing to their sensuality. Settembrini, however, does not see the conflict between spirit and nature. Rather, the main problem threatening the harmony of the individual is the conflict between individual and community interests. Political systems should represent the will of all individuals and be made more humane, so as to eliminate the causes of human suffering.

At this stage, Castorp, like Haller, functions as the representative of the German cultural tradition. Castorp is himself the prize in the intellectual contest between East and West, just as Mann defines Germany as the battleground of European antinomies (Mann, *GW* 12: 54). Soon Castorp will come to his own conclusion on the meaning of life. In so doing, he gives a definition of the relationship between the individual and the community which amounts to a restatement of Mann's notion of humanity. Appropriately enough, Castorp finds the meaning of life by returning to the Romantic realm of vision, which, as I noted in the comparison of *Der Tod in Venedig* and *Der Steppenwolf*, is linked to the somatic domain.

5.8 Crane Dance in the Snow: Ascent up the Mountain

Although he continues to learn through his discussions with Naphta and Settembrini, Castorp does not find the meaning of life until he extends his path into the realm of vision. Previously, Castorp had gone to the wooded grove where he dreamed of Hippe, and returned there to contemplate his experiences in his sleepy, pious state. These comprise his "Regierungsgeschäfte." This path, then, is a way out of the sanatorium labyrinth and is associated with death and Romantic forces in Castorp, i.e., the sympathy with death and his inner visions. In the chapter "Schnee," Castorp moves past the grove to the snow-covered mountaintop where he has the dream which enables him to understand human existence in terms of corporality. Castorp ascends the mountain in a Crane Dance pattern; he goes in a spiral in the snow until he stops and faces death. Both phases of this process are indicated by the term "umkommen" (literally to come around or figuratively to die), the term which Castorp uses to designate his movement. After the dream, light appears in the sky. Castorp then reverses his direction and returns to the sanatorium.

By taking the path to the light, Castorp gains the knowledge to redefine his stance towards Settembrini and Naphta and also to break the hold of the sympathy with death. Hence, it is only fitting that at the beginning of Castorp's ascent, Castorp metaphorically moves away from Western thinking and towards Romanticism. He recalls Settembrini's warning on "Walpurgisnacht," "Eh, Ingegnere, un po' di ragione, sa!" (Mann, *GW* 3: 660), and compares the blue light left in the snow by his ski poles with that of Clavdia's eyes. The connection between Clavdia, the object of Castorp's desire, and snow, a product of nature, indicates that Castorp is embarking on an exploration of nature and human nature, the domain of the body. This idea is reinforced by Castorp's comparison of the snow to the sea.

He is reminded of Sylt where he once stood at the edge of the powerful waves. This was an early experience with the deadly power of nature which entrances Castorp:

Von dorther kannte der junge Mensch das Begeisterungsglück leichter Liebesberührungen mit Mächten, deren volle Umarmung vernichtend sein würde. Was er aber nicht gekannt hatte, war die Neigung, diese begeisternde Berührung mit der tödlichen Natur so weit zu verstärken, daß die volle Umarmung drohte.... (Mann, *GW* 3: 658)

His fascination with the sea stems from his "Sympathie mit den Elementen" (Mann, *GW* 3: 659). Hence, the motifs of death and eros recur in his relationship to nature. Both the sea and the snow represent the deadly, chaotic power of nature.

The snow and clouds serve further as a link to the German cultural tradition. Clouds appear in conjunction with Castorp's first movement to the grove, when he recalls his passion for Hippe, and later in his recollection of his boat ride. In both cases, the clouds provide information about German Romanticism. On this occasion, the clouds and snow are used to represent Schopenhauer's nothingness. In point of fact, the term "nichts" appears twice during Castorp's ascent. The Romantics and Schopenhauer both believe that there is a metaphysical unity behind phenomenal appearances. On the snowy mountain peak Castorp's perceptions of space and time, the Schopenhauerian basis for individuation, become unclear. He looks at his watch three times only to discover with surprise how little time has elapsed. It is also difficult to perceive spatial relations in the snowy darkness. Castorp moves upward to terraces of the mountain, whose "...obere Regionen verschwamm mit dem Himmel, der ebenso nebelweiß war wie sie" (Mann, *GW* 3: 660). Eventually Castorp's space is reduced to the place where he stands at the hut. He cannot move any closer to the wall and the wind prevents him from leaving.

Additionally, Castorp encounters "Urschweigen" (Mann, *GW* 3: 657) and "Leere" (Mann, *GW* 3: 661) on his spiral path to the hut. In Dierks' opinion, Castorp moves through the snow ("weißliche Transzendenz") and "das Nichts" to the point where he undergoes the metaphysical negation of the individual in Schopenhauerian terms (Dierks 123-124).[14] When Castorp finally stops at the hut, the wind blows at him like "Sensen" or scythes, a veiled allusion to Hippe. Castorp can develop an intellectual response to the forces of disease that first manifested themselves in his dream of Hippe, or he can succumb to them and perish. Castorp's spiral movement towards death closely resembles Haller's pattern of movement on the night when he meets Hermine. In Castorp's case, the encounter with death offers a twofold prospect of transcendence. He could succumb to the sympathy with death, a dangerous wish to exist on a higher plane of being. On the other hand, he could attain a kind of self-transcendence by overcoming the deadly forces of disease and developing an understanding of human existence. Castorp decides not to lie down to rest because he would certainly perish. Subsequently, the great soul in Castorp, a deep cultural imprint that combines societal and individual memories, has its dream. In terms of Schopenhauer's philosophy, Castorp is experiencing a mystical "nunc stans...ein stehendes Jetzt ungetrübter und ewiger Ideen" (Mann, *GW* 12: 539) through which the individual can apperceive the fundamental unity of being beneath the surface of empirical reality.

Through the dream, Castorp gains a new understanding of his experiences on the mountain. Some critics have tried to identify the source for the settings and landscapes of the dream. Most researchers have concentrated on the last two scenes of the dream, the episodes with the people of the sun and the witches at the temple. The sources of the dream have variously been identified as Ludwig von Hofmann's paintings "Die Quelle" and "Der Frühling,"[15] Goethe's diary entries during his stay in Italy,[16] and *Faust* II, especially Faust's trip to the mothers.[17]

Dierks and Peter Pütz[18] maintain that the vision objectifies the Apollonian and Dionysian, two contrasting patterns of thought that can be seen as responses to corporality. The contrast between the beauty of the people of the sun and the horrors of the cannibalistic ritual in the temple is the conflict between the Apollonian and Dionysian cultures as Nietzsche described them (Dierks 125). I share their view, but I would also argue that most of the previous interpretations of the dream have not adequately focused on the connection between the configurations in the chapter "Schnee" and other sections of the work. These links shed a new light on the German tradition.

In the first landscape, Castorp has a totality of sensual experience ("Synästhie") common to the Romantics and Goethe (Lehnert 11). Castorp compares the rainbow to the singing of an Italian tenor he enjoys. In the second scene, he sits on steps on a mountain as he gazes down at the people of the sun. The boy who points behind him interrupts Castorp's rapture. Since the boy with the "deadly resolute" face directs Castorp to a scene of horror, we can consider the boy to be the *Todesgenius*, the depiction of death in Greek culture as literary figures of eighteenth-century Germany saw him.[19] His pose is similar to that of Tadzio as he stands on the beach in Aschenbach's final moments. Castorp makes his way to the temple, where inside two witches devour a blond child whose head they hold over a bowl.

The last two scenes represent the Apollonian and Dionysian. E. M. Butler[20] argues that while the terms are most often associated with Nietzsche, they are also in accord with the allusions to Goethe:

Goethe...finally confessed to a daimonic element which came over him at times and forced him to do its will...Nietzsche called this element Dionysian, and described it as the shattering of the bonds of the individual who becomes merged in the spirit of universal life. (Butler 87)

Goethe acutely felt the pull between the Dionysian and Apollonian in Naples, especially as he looked out to the sea:

Cautiously he admitted the sensation of infinite space, pulling himself back again almost immediately to study the shapes of the waves in a storm; trying to ban the daimonic, Dionysian element into Apolline form. (Butler 111)

Significantly, the people in the dream stand before the sea. The sea is a cipher for death, chaos and the power of nature, uncontrollable forces of life in *Der Zauberberg*.[21]   Likewise, Nietzsche defines the Dionysian and Apollonian cultures as responses to the horrors of life. The Apollonian tries to overcome the separation from nature, the source of our bodily being, through religion; whereas the Dionysian seeks a mystical return to nature. Hence, both are reactions to fundamental *Lebensangst*, especially the dread of death. The presence of the euphemistic *Todesgenius* among the people of the sun would signal an attempt to tame the fear. The people of the sun represent the Western Enlightenment, and, given the allusions to Goethe, the ideals of Classicism: the embodied idea, beauty, dignity and virtuousness. In contrast, the witches represent aspects of Romanticism. Nietzsche's analysis points to several common features shared by the Dionysian and Romanticism: the influence of the East, lust, intoxication, and the striving towards unity among individuals, and between nature and humanity. The connection between the Romantic and the Dionysian is treated by Mann in "Pariser Rechenschaft":

Das Stammelement des "sinnlichen" spielt eine größere Rolle darin, und zwar einer zum Rausch und zum Untergang geneigten Sinnlichkeit, des Romantisch-Dionysischen also: der Begriff umfaßt den Komplex von Schönheit, Lust und Tod als Gegensatz zu dem von Zucht, Ordnung, Klarheit, Vernunft, Moral.... (Mann, *GW* 11: 77)

In his interpretation of the vision, Castorp identifies the people of the sun with Settembrini's thinking, and the witches with Naphta's. Castorp rejects the stances of both figures since both, in their own way, give one-sided interpretations of life, especially with respect to the polarity life-death. "Tod oder Leben—Krankheit, Gesundheit—Geist und Natur. Sind das wohl Widersprüche? Ich frage: sind das Fragen? Nein..." (Mann, *GW* 3: 685). In further discussing the views of Naphta and Settembrini, Castorp redefines humanity, the core idea of Mann's concept of community. For Castorp, life and death are part of a higher entity: the human individual. "Der Mensch ist Herr der Gegensätze, sie sind durch ihn, und also ist er vornehmer als sie" (Mann, *GW* 3: 685). Death, Castorp concludes, can be prevented from becoming an autonomous spiritual force only through the power of love. His relationship to other individuals should therefore be based on love:

> Ich will mich hell erinnern, daß Treue zum Tode und Gewesenen nur Bosheit...und Menschenfeindschaft ist, bestimmt sie unser Denken und Regieren. *Der Mensch soll um der Güte und Liebe willen dem Tode keine Herrschaft einräumen über seine Gedanken.* (Mann, *GW* 3: 686)

It is significant that Castorp develops his understanding of life by having a vision much like Gustav von Aschenbach and Haller in the Magic Theater. In all three texts, sensuality opens the way to the realm of vision. In Castorp's case, it is his erotic desire, as evidenced by the references to Hippe and Clavdia, that draws him into the realm of vision in the snowy reaches of the mountain. Thus, it is his desire for the body which eventually enables him to understand life.

Castorp's interpretation can be traced back to the new relationship between love and death which evolved in Mann's thinking as he completed *Der Zauberberg* in the early 1920s. It is true that in *Betrachtungen eines Unpolitischen* (1918), Mann links humanity with the sympathy with death and with sympathy ("Mitleid") but not to "Liebe" (love) and "Güte" (goodness). But in his essay "Schopenhauer" from 1938, Mann maintains that "love" and "goodness" are constituent elements of the ethics of Schopenhauer whom Mann considers as the quintessential German philosopher. "Liebe und Güte sind *Mitleid*, aus der Erkenntnis des 'Tat twam asi', der Lüftung des Maja-Schleiers..." (Mann, *GW* 9: 554). Mann explains elsewhere in the essay that the various phenomena of the (empirical) world are part of the veil of Maya that conceals the essential unity of all entities and of all individuals. Hence, Mann speaks of the illusory difference between "Ich" and "Du." From this unity, Mann derives his understanding of the "Mitleid" of one individual for another: "Denn ein Mensch solcher Liebeserkenntnis wird das Leiden aller Lebenden als das seine betrachten" (Mann, *GW* 12: 555). Thus, sympathy remains part of humanity from 1918 to 1938, but love and goodness are synonyms for sympathy only after the completion of the *Betrachtungen* and are therefore new components of humanity. Appropriately enough, humanity is also congruent with Schopenhauer's notion that the body of an individual is part of Maya, a manifestation of the common will. In a sense, Hans Castorp effectively restates Mann's concept of humanity in his interpretation of the dream.

The appearance of light in half of the sky signifies Castorp's newly found understanding of life. With respect to Castorp, the light appears as the figure avows *Liebe* and *Güte*, the Classical affirmation of life along the lines of Meister's *Lebensdienst*, as an antidote to the Romantic sympathy with death. Effectively, the figure frees the sympathy with the organic from disease. In this context, the presence of light does not indicate Mann's affirmation of Enlightenment thinking.[22] After all, Castorp sets out by moving away from Settembrini. Rather, the light indicates a higher degree of insight that comes from affirming contradictions in life. ("Der Mensch ist Herr der Gegensätze.") By the same token, the contrasting pattern of light-dark (clouds) in the sky must be seen in terms of Mann's striving to locate an underlying unity between Classicism and Romanticism in the early 1920s. Two figures from German cultural history who, according to Mann, achieve this difficult synthesis are, significantly, Goethe and Schopenhauer (Mann, *GW* 9: 576).

In short, Castorp takes the path out of the labyrinth and develops an understanding of life. His interpretation of the dream gives him new insights into ontological issues. At the same time, the dream can be understood as a reinterpretation of the cultural tradition of Germany in terms of corporality. The challenge for Castorp now is to use his insight in the real world so as to remedy the effects of the cultural crisis.

5.9 Politicization of the Sanatorium Labyrinth

In the chapter "Schnee," Castorp appears to find the meaning of life. In his statements after the dream he affirms human love, a concerned engagement for others, and rejects death. Castorp gains understanding, as signified by the motif of the light, by taking the path out of the sanatorium labyrinth. The next phase of the Crane Dance is the movement towards new life. Castorp, however, goes back to the diseased world of the sanatorium where his dream fades from his memory.

Indeed, he begins to forget the dream the next day. Kristiansen sees this as a sign that the Dionysian realm, including the sympathy with death, cannot be brought under intellectual control.[23] This foreshadows the eventual triumph of the Dionysian irrational with the outbreak of the First World War (Kristiansen 296). Koopmann, on the other hand, argues that there are indications that Castorp overcomes the sympathy with death. Castorp distances himself from Naphta when he describes the grave as the site of alchemistic transmutation in terms which echo his experiences in the snow (Koopmann, *KMR* 59-60). Further, Castorp incisively recognizes his cousin's animal-like innocence in the face of death and quickly discerns Peeperkorn's existential fear behind the celebrations of life. I therefore share Koopmann's view that Castorp does not completely forget the lessons of the dream.

But Koopmann's observation does not explain why Castorp stays at the sanatorium. The answer is, I would argue, that Castorp returns to the labyrinth to face a new challenge. He must develop his understanding of life into a political notion of community. The motif of the labyrinth establishes a causal relationship between the cultural crisis depicted in *Der Tod in Venedig* and *Der Zauberberg* and the First World War as it is presented in *Der Zauberberg*. The danger in the Venice and sanatorium labyrinths is comprised by death and eros, the diseased sympathy with the organic, which is a response to human corporality. For Castorp, the key to finding the path to the light is the expansion of his ability to love; in this respect, the configurations of *Der Zauberberg* match those of Hesse's *Steppenwolf*. In Castorp's case, the quester figure develops an understanding of life that is essentially a restatement of Mann's concept of humanity, a form of human love. To be sure, the themes of love, eros, and death are in no way inherently political. But a close analysis of the thematic patterns shows that the fields of meaning of these themes grow to include politics in the final chapter. This is the primary cause of the politicization of the sanatorium labyrinth. In section 5.10, I show that the sanatorium labyrinth, as well as the themes of love, death, and eros recur on the battlefield, a place of military-political conflict. If the labyrinth is a challenge of existential orientation, then the war labyrinth is a challenge of existential and political orientation.

This represents a significant change in the nature of Castorp's quest, but can be explained by examining Mann's thoughts on culture and politics during the period in which he worked on *Der Zauberberg*. In Mann's 1912 novella *Der Tod in Venedig*, death and eros appear in conjunction with the Dionysian and the East. In the chapter "Kahnfahrt" of the 1924 novel *Der Zauberberg*, Castorp's associations establish a link between death, eros and the German

Romantic tradition. Before and during the First World War, Mann argues that the German cultural tradition is unpolitical. Still, Mann's concern about the politicization of German cultural life is one of the predominant topics of *Betrachtungen eines Unpolitischen* (1918). But after the war, it was clear to conservative intellectuals such as Mann that life in Germany was becoming politicized.[24] Worse yet, militant reactionaries threatened to use Romanticism for their own agenda. Mann's struggle with politics was in no small part set in motion by the potential appropriation of the Romantic tradition. Since they make use of a tradition whose integral elements are, according to Mann, death and eros, their ideology can be identified with Naphta's terroristic mysticism and with the sympathy with death. Additionally, Naphta is of course a figure from the East, and in his essays from the 1920s such as "Goethe und Tolstoi," Mann likens the reactionaries in Germany to their authoritarian counterparts in the East: the Communists in the newly founded Soviet Union. Hence, from Mann's own writings, it is possible to place the human love-sympathy with death dialectic in a political framework.   In *Der Zauberberg*, the cultural crisis culminates in a political catastrophe, the First World War. Signs of death, eros, and disease in the flatlands connect the cultural crisis with the coming war. As I pointed out in section 5.3, the lack of any real purpose for work afflicts individuals in Europe with a kind of disease. Although Castorp is on the mountain for most of the text, there are still allusions to death and eros in the music Castorp hears from the lowlands in Europe throughout the text: military marches and *Carmen*. The marches are preludes to the First World War, and *Carmen* the story of a femme fatale who brings a soldier to ruin. Thus, the diseased sympathy with the organic is present in Europe and on the mountain alike. In the chapter "Fülle des Wohllauts" Castorp himself grows interested in music replete with references to death and eros. He quickly becomes the keeper of the new gramophone and plays selected works, such as the aforementioned *Carmen*. His favorite work is Schubert's "Lindenbaum." The narrator comments at length on the political implications of the song. On one level, Castorp's fascination with the song may well express his desire to go back to Germany where he can use his knowledge to improve the world. The song concerns a Romantic wanderer on his way home. At the same time, Castorp's love of the song, a product of the sympathy with death, is an ominous sign. In his comments on the political implications of the song, the narrator in *Der Zauberberg* wonders whether the sympathy with death can be countered by love:

Man mochte wahrscheinlich sogar Reiche darauf gründen, irdisch-allzu-irdische Reiche, sehr derb und fortschrittsfroh...in welchen das Lied zur elektrischen Grammophonmusik verdarb. Aber sein bester Sohn mochte doch derjenige sein, der in seiner Überwindung sein Leben verzehrte und starb, auf den Lippen das neue Wort der Liebe, das er noch nicht zu sprechen wußte.... (Mann, *GW* 3: 907)

For Mann, Schubert's song was a codeword for the political reaction in the 1920s.[25] In Mann's critique in "Pariser Rechenschaft," the reactionary expropriation of Schubert's wanderer ties together two deadly elements: the "philosophy of brutality" and the sympathy with death (Mann, *GW* 11: 21). This observation echoes Mann's comments on the anti-Western conservatism of the Heidelberg Romantics in "Pariser Rechenschaft" in which Mann joins their patriotic longing for the past in a nexus with death and eros. It must be emphasized that the sympathy with death must be countered by the new word of love. Given the antagonism between love (or humanity) and the diseased sympathy with the organic, love must also have a political dimension.

On a philosophical plane, Castorp's concept of love as humanity counters this insidious sympathy. Thus, a political concept of humanity would counter the politicized Romantic sympathy with death. In "Geist und Wesen der Republik," Mann himself argues that the German concept of humanity must be expanded to encompass politics. "Der deutsche Mensch...steht vor der Einsicht, daß er...seinen Bildungs-, Kultur- und Humanitätsbegriff zu früh geschlossen hat, als er das politische Element,...den republikanischen Gedanken davon abschloß..." (Mann, *GW* 9: 856). But Castorp does not actually articulate his own political position based on the knowledge he gains on the snow-covered mountain. In his interpretation of the dream, Castorp clearly articulates his own philosophical view of life. Further, he situates himself politically between Settembrini and Naphta; "...in der Mitte ist des Homo Dei Stand--inmitten zwischen mystischer Durchgängerei und Vernunft--wie auch sein Staat ist zwischen mystischer Gemeinschaft und windigem Einzeltum" (Mann, *GW* 3: 685). Although Castorp effectively redefines humanity, he fails to develop a political concept of love because he stops attending to his reflective "Regierungsgeschäfte." The term means governmental affairs, but Castorp never actually reflects on his own political stance in his visits to the grove or after the dream in the snow. As a result, Castorp does not know the new word of love to counter the political form of the sympathy with death expressed later in Schubert's "Lindenbaum." This dialectic between love and disease holds the key to the battlefield scene.

Similarly, the patients' moral disease begins to develop political complications near the end of the text. In the analysis of *Der Prozeß*, I argued that Josef K.'s aggression has libidinal roots and is a symptom of his reified way of being, a condition which applies to the patients as well. In the chapter "Die große Gereiztheit," incidents of aggression begin to occur. The patients become irritable, attack each other in conversation, and, in one case, have a fist fight in the hallway. These actions are not inherently political, but they do mirror the growing tension in antebellum Europe. The exchange of letters preceding the fisticuffs in the hallway foreshadows the exchange of diplomatic communiques in the summer of 1914. In this sense, there is a political dimension to the aggression among the patients. Since the hostilities take place at Berghof, the sanatorium becomes politicized. The sanatorium, a place of reflection, mirrors the political tension which eventually results in the catastrophe.

The climax of the hostilities is the duel between Naphta and Settembrini. Significantly, the place of their duel is the very same Romantic wooded grove where Castorp had once dreamed of Hippe.[26] Later, he attends his "Regierungsgeschäfte" up on the mountain as he contemplates his experiences on the mountain including the debates between Naphta and Settembrini. Eventually, Castorp takes this path to the realm of vision and develops his own understanding of life in contradistinction to those of Settembrini and Naphta. The space with allusions to Novalis's realm of unity (the blue flower) is now the site of armed political conflict. Hence, the politicization of Berghof has such a powerful impact that it ravages the Romantic spaces in which Castorp learns through visions. The destruction of those places is captured by the barren snowscape in what was once the wooded grove. Because Naphta and Settembrini represent both German and European ideologies, their duel in the grove indicates that the European conflagration triggers political conflicts in Germany from which the unpolitical German cultural tradition cannot emerge unscathed.

Thus, not only the sanatorium labyrinth but also the realm of vision are transformed into spaces where political disputes turn violent. These disputes are the result of forces which Castorp has already confronted, though not on a political plane. Castorp is again challenged to find his intellectual orientation in the recurrence of the politicized labyrinth, the battlefield.

5.10 War-Labyrinth

I would argue that by analyzing the representation of the battlefield as a labyrinth, or more precisely as a variation of the sanatorium labyrinth, new insights can be gained into the last chapter of Mann's *Zauberberg*. The recurrence of the sanatorium labyrinth shows that the cultural crisis captured by the world at Berghof ultimately results in the First World War. The lowlands where the battlefield labyrinth appears are also marked by this dangerous sympathy. Thus, once again Castorp the quester figure must orient himself towards human corporality, but this time, in a labyrinth formed by political conflict. Castorp, as I will show, embodies two conflicting possibilities for Romanticism. I suggest that the fact that Castorp is not definitively aligned with either option reflects Mann's uncertainty about the direction of the Romantic tradition in the early 1920s.

The person-space configurations of the mountain are mirrored on the battlefield. Castorp arrives at both places after a train ride. The magical number seven recurs as Castorp's unit must march seven hours. Their march is "kein Lustwandel," the term used for the walks Castorp and Joachim take at Davos. On the mountain there is the town of Davos which is joined to the sanatorium by a road. A second road branches off into the woods. On the battlefield, there is a burning village near hills and a road from which a second road forks off into the nearby forest.

The recurrences do not stop there. On the contrary, the battlefield, like the sanatorium, is a place of eros, disease, and death. Young people from all over Europe appear at Berghof and on the battlefield. Moreover, the soldiers, like the patients are diseased. The narrator states that Castorp's army unit is composed of "die dreitausend fiebernden Knaben" (Mann, *GW* 3: 991). The narrator in *Der Zauberberg* does not make a direct reference to an erotic relationship among the soldiers. But in *Betrachtungen eines Unpolitischen*, Mann argues that the individual has a mystical experience of love in war: "Jedermann fühlt und weiß, daß im Krieg ein mystisches Element enthalten ist: es ist dasselbe, das allen Grundmächten des Lebens, der Zeugung und dem Tode, der Religion und der Liebe eignet" (Mann, *GW* 12: 464). In his essay "Von deutscher Republik," Mann expands on this idea by quoting Goethe. "Heißt es nicht, daß der Krieg mit seinen Erlebnissen von Blut- und Todeskameradschaft, der harten und ausschließlichen Männlichkeit seiner Lebensform und Atmosphäre das Reich dieses Eros mächtig verstärkt habe?" (Mann, *GW* 11: 848). Finally, diseased patients from all over Europe are confined to a world of death at the sanatorium, just as the troops on the battlefield are trapped in a "Weltfest des Todes." In short, the world of Berghof reappears in varied form on the battlefield.

Missing is only the sanatorium, the labyrinthine building. Based on the recurrence of the spatial pattern of mountain, it is possible to conclude that war itself is the labyrinth. For both labyrinths in physical space, disease is the path inside. On the battlefield, Castorp again sings Schubert's "Lindenbaum," which the narrator sees as a symptom of a dangerous "Rückneigung." It is therefore this form of disease, the Romantic affinity for lost worlds, that leads him into the most menacing labyrinth of all. In the war labyrinth, the motif of the body recurs as well. On the mountain, one of the most important objects of study for Castorp is the human body, which like society, is organized on the principal of division of labor (Mann, *GW* 3: 395-396). Likewise Castorp's unit is "ein Körper, darauf berechnet, nach großen Ausfällen noch handeln und siegen...zu können..." (Mann, *GW* 3: 991). The polarity individual-community is defined in Mann's notion of humanity. In this case, the relationship between the individual (soldier) and the community (unit) is defined in terms of the body in an unambiguously political context. Implicitly, the quester figure of Castorp is called upon to make his way through a political labyrinth by expanding his understanding of human embodiment.

Labyrinths in general are a challenge of orientation and finding order in chaos. In the war, however, it is impossible to determine any direction at all. "Hier ist ein Wegweiser, -unnütz ihn zu befragen; Halbdunkel würde uns seine Schrift verhüllen, auch wenn das Schild nicht von einem Durchschlag zackig zerissen wäre. Ost oder West?" (Mann, *GW* 3: 990). Finding a path between East and West, a central question in Castorp's intellectual labyrinth, is out of the question. When Castorp does find the middle philosophical position in "Schnee", the sun breaks through the clouds. Now the "trübe" sky is covered with rain clouds. The landscape is ravaged to the point where the road is indistinguishable from the woods. In the war labyrinth, nature and civilization are threatened with complete destruction.

In the end, Castorp leaves the sanatorium labyrinth, the realm of reflection on the mountain, and enters a far more deadly labyrinth in the real world. In this respect, the conclusion of *Der Zauberberg* is comparable to that of Hesse's *Steppenwolf*. Both Castorp and Haller are representatives of Germany who are challenged to use their insights in the real world. On this level of signification, Castorp's orientation in the war labyrinth furnishes information about the shape of the world, or more specifically the post-war world, since *Der Zauberberg* was completed in 1924. The parameters for

Castorp's orientation in the war labyrinth are the same poles of humanity and the sympathy with death that occur on the mountain.

For Castorp the key to overcoming the forces of disease on the mountain is the encounter with death. In his perilous adventure in the snow, he resists the temptation to die and eventually develops a new understanding of human love. Similarly, Mann discusses how individuals can overcome dangerous Romantic forces with which they identify. In his essay "Vorspruch zu einer musikalischen Nietzsche-Feier,"[27] Mann describes how Nietzsche achieves this kind of self-transcendence:

> Dies ist er uns: ...ein Freund des Lebens...ein Lehrer der Überwindung all dessen in uns, was dem Leben und der Zukunft entgegensteht, das heißt des Romantischen. Denn das Romantische ist das Lied des Heimwehs nach dem Vergangenen, das Zauberberlied des Todes.... (Mann, *GW* 10: 182)

It is surely no coincidence that the narrator uses nearly identical words to discuss ways of conquering the *Rückneigung* expressed in Schubert's "Lindenbaum."[28] In this context, Castorp's singing of the song on the battlefield must be seen as a warning concerning the politics of the 1920s. If individuals do not overcome sympathy with death, they will be susceptible to the siren song of the reactionaries. Their policies, the conclusion of the text shows, will result in military catastrophe and death. In this dismal situation, the narrator of *Der Zauberberg* wonders whether a world of love will emerge from the ashes of war. This statement echoes the narrator's hope that individuals who overcome the Romantic sympathy with death expressed in Schubert's "Lindenbaum" will find the new word of love. The term love is left rather vague in *Der Zauberberg*, and this can be attributed to Mann's difficulty in finding an appropriate political form for humanity. In his "Von deutscher Republik," Mann himself presents the Weimar Republic as the political form of humanity.

To be sure, Mann had an uneasy reconciliation with the Weimar Republic and was often critical of it. He eventually made his peace with the Republic, in large part for fear of nationalistic reactionaries, some of whom were using the Romantic tradition for their own agenda. Eventually, Mann endorsed the Weimar Republic in public addresses such as "Von deutscher Republik" as a shield against the reactionaries. Mann, in fact, delivered "Von deutscher Republik" to reactionary students, many of whom served in the war. Mann inscribes the Weimar Republic into his dialectical schema of the humanity versus sympathy with death. Mann argues that the Weimar Republic is the realization of Novalis's concept of humanity; similarly, Berman asserts that Mann advocates a kind of Romantic community in this address (269). According to Mann, Novalis's concept of humanity is "ein anderes Wort, ein politisches" for the Republic (Mann, *GW* 11: 844). Since the basis of humanity is love (Mann, *GW* 11: 844), democracy must by definition be based on love. Since democracy is equated with humanity, the Weimar Republic is defined as Mann's older conception of an idealized community; it is an aesthetic community in which individuals are joined in love.

Additionally, both humanity and the Republic have the same function in "Von deutscher Republik" as love does in Castorp's interpretation of the dream in the snow. Humanity occupies the middle ground between "Mystik und Ratio" (Mann, *GW* 11: 830) just as the Republic is equally "entfernt...von der politischen Mystik des Slawentums...wie von anarchischen Radikal-Individualismus eines gewissen Westens" (Mann, *GW* 11: 835). These statements echo Castorp's rejection of the philosophies of Naphta and Settembrini in favor of love of the individual. Finally, love is the element which unifies antinomies at the end of Heinrich von Ofterdingen's journey. Likewise, the Weimar Republic harmonizes antinomies, above all the pair state-culture (Mann, *GW* 11: 827).

The contradictory political implications of Castorp's appearance on the battlefield make earlier interpretative judgements of the conclusion more difficult to maintain. Hans Mayer concludes that the way from death and decay to democracy and life goes through the trenches.[29] But there is no clear indication that Castorp risks his life for the "new word of love," to paraphrase the narrator, for the battlefield is also a space of disease and death. Conversely, the text does not, as Kristiansen argues, represent the collapse of civilization into barbarism; the narrator still identifies love as a possible means of renewal. Castorp could potentially go either way. He is challenged to orient himself in the war labyrinth much as he did on the mountain. Castorp's movement through a political labyrinth indicates that the solution of the cultural crisis depicted in the text depends on the political orientation of the quester. Mann may well have left the conclusion of the text open in order to challenge his readers: the final chapter of his *Zauberberg* suggest that the cultural life of Germany hinges on whether the readers can resist the political sympathy with death.

CHAPTER 6

Conclusion

The motif of the labyrinth has throughout its long history served as a cipher for confusion. City labyrinths in literature from the late nineteenth and early twentieth centuries capture the paradox of modernization in Europe. In the eighteenth and nineteenth centuries, it was widely believed that reason would ensure progress to a better, if not more perfect, world. The products of reason, social, economic, and scientific progress, brought about unprecedented change in Europe in the nineteenth century, change which was manifest in cities rapidly undergoing irreversible transformations. In Germany, impoverished peasants began to stream from the country to the cities in the mid-nineteenth century, and the flow accelerated after German unification. Modernization eventually gave rise to mass social forms and bureaucratic (rational) planning as a way of giving order to social life. These developments caused unease among some intellectuals. George Mosse[1] has analyzed the reaction of German cultural conservatives to economic progress and the concomitant decline of traditional agrarian social structure in the nineteenth century. For the conservatives, the city was a metonymy for the ills of modernization. The dark view of the city was by no means confined to conservative observers. Expressionist poetry abounds with images of menacing, destructive cities. Negative conceptions of the modern city such as these are part of a broader cultural current: the suspicion of the ideology of progress and especially of the societal use of reason. This intellectual tendency can be seen in Max Weber's attack on modern bureaucracy, Nietzsche' broadsides against rational scientific thinking, and Georg Simmel's critique of the monetary economy. In this context, it is easy to see why modern cities would be depicted as a labyrinth, as a mythological underworld. The labyrinth captures the cultural and social disorientation triggered by modernization. Indeed, the city labyrinth suggests that modern individuals have become trapped in a hellish world of their own creation.

In short, it is my contention that the modern city labyrinth in literature is aligned with forces which were thought to be undermining traditional social and cultural relations. A tool for tracking this process is Eagleton's concept of aesthetics in bourgeois society as a discourse of the body. Eagleton's notion is a useful starting point for examining various conceptions of the intellectual relationship to the body. Having a material relationship to the body precludes the success of the quester's search. The themes which signify a material relationship to the body are lust (a form of eros), aggression, and the dread of death. The patterns which characterize an intellectual relationship to corporality can only be derived from isolated actions of marginal figures in *Der Prozeß*, and from patterns in other works by Kafka. An intellectual relationship to the body encompasses the capacity for reflection, showing committed concern for others (a kind of caritas), and the ability to anticipate and acknowledge death. The contrasting patterns of light and darkness are inscribed into this dialectical structure. Figures with an intellectual relationship to the somatic domain can find the path to the light. But K., who has a material way of being, continually moves down the same paths and becomes disoriented in the darkness. Finding the way to the light is a conventional metaphor for gaining understanding, but it is also a vehicle for presenting a modern issue: the relationship between the text and desire. The figures' efforts to find the meaning of life must be sustained by the desire to understand life in terms of the body, and after gaining the insights to interpret being, they must present their views in a written text. Most figures, however, have a material orientation and are therefore incapable of producing a meaningful text. K. utterly fails to finish a text, an error that seals his doom. The conception of the figures, above all of K., reveals Kafka's deep skepticism about the possibility of establishing a new way of relating to the body and, by extension, new cultural codes.

By contrast, Mann and Hesse explore the possibility of redefining Classic-Romantic aesthetic codes and renewing them for modern culture. Still, some of the same thematic patterns occur in all three texts. In Hesse's *Steppenwolf* and Mann's *Zauberberg*, agression and the dread of death appear with respect to figures who are either lost in darkness (Haller) or are confined in a labyrinth (the patients in the sanatorium). Like Josef K., the patients succumb to uncontrollable sensuous impulses and have a reified way of being. But in the end, the intellectually curious quester figures, Haller and Castorp, do move toward the light. In contrast to K., they do not shy away from the encounter with death and are willing to test new and unfamiliar paths. Consequently, Haller and Castorp enjoy tremendous intellectual growth. The key to this process is eros. More precisely, the key is a form of eros that is capable of being enhanced so that the figure experiences higher stages of love and, simultaneously, higher planes of knowledge. That eros plays a crucial role in the intellectual and personal development of Haller and Castorp shows that it has a much different function in *Der Steppenwolf* and *Der Zauberberg* than in *Der Prozeß*. The discourse of the body in Hesse's *Steppenwolf* and Mann's *Zauberberg* is not dialectically structured but is instead built on a series of polarities. In Hesse's text, eros establishes harmony among such polarities as male-female, man-wolf, and spirit-nature. In Mann's *Zauberberg*, eros can be a dangerous force when it appears in conjunction with reification or as part of the sympathy with death. But Castorp experiences a form of eros which actually fuels his desire for knowledge and prevents him from falling prey to these dangers; his intellectual stance on life effectively is based on erotic desire that has been cleansed of diseased elements. Effectively, Castorp articulates a reinterpretation of humanity, a spiritualized form of eros rooted in the sympathy with the organic; humanity serves essentially the same purpose as eros does in *Der Steppenwolf* in that it represents a higher unity among philosophical and existential antinomies. Finally, it should be emphasized that eros can play a constructive role in the development of quester figures, provided that they are capable of reflecting on sensuous or bodily experiences.

In other words, the sensuous experience of the body provides the figures with the material for intellectually engaging their existence as embodied subjects. The discourse of the body in *Der Steppenwolf* and *Der Zauberberg* includes cultural reflection. Indeed, the body is the integral element in reinterpreting the cultural tradition. For Haller, erotic encounters with women enable him to understand the spirit expressed in the works of the great cultural figures whom he admires. At the same time, these encounters represent the joining of spirit with nature, a central concern in the idealist aesthetic tradition with which he identifies. In Mann's *Zauberberg*, the body functions as a metonymy of cultural traditions, as the discussions of the pietá between Naphta and Settembrini illustrate. For Castorp, Settembrini's grandfather literally embodies the Western Enlightenment, just as his own grandfather embodies German Romanticism.

There is an additional aspect of corporality which Mann's text shares with Hesse's. Eros draws the figures onto the path to the light, a path that leads to the realm of vision in the Magic Theater and to the snowy moutaintop respectively. The realm of vision is an objectification of the figures' unconscious; the connection between the unconscious and the domain of the body is hardly unique to these texts and clearly stands in opposition to older conceptions of the rational conscious subject. Eros effectively opens the way to the mystical realm of vision in which personal memories and cultural imprints are combined. By having a mystical vision, the figures gain the insight necessary to understand their own lives and to reinterpret the cultural tradition—in short, to renew the idealist aesthetic tradition.

The Magic Theater points to another aspect of the motif of the labyrinth common to all three texts. In each work, there is, in addition to the city labyrinth, a labyrinth of reflection: the hermeneutical labyrinth in *Der Prozeß*, the Magic Theater, and the intellectual labyrinth which Castorp traverses on his visits with Behrens, Naphta, and Settembrini. The recurrence of the motif of the labyrinth on a plane of reflection shows that the cultural crisis, as represented by the city, shapes ways in which the depicted civilization interprets itself. Further, corporality is the determining factor in the questers' progress in the labyrinth of reflection. In Kafka's *Prozeß*, the conflicting interpretations of the parable form the hermeneutical labyrinth. K. utterly fails to engage in substantive exchanges of meaning, the precondition of developing an interpretation. This can be traced back to his inability to anticipate death. Thus, K. gets lost in the hermeneutical labyrinth, and this is an ominous sign since K. owes his success in part to his ability to interpret business texts. Kafka is saying that most individuals do not understand the cultural tradition and are incapable of developing a new idea of social or cultural relations in the modern world.

By contrast, the movement of Harry Haller through the Magic Theater shows how modern civilization can be intellectually guided on the basis of renewed idealist aesthetic codes. As Haller develops under Hermine's tutelage, he begins to attain psychic wholeness. This can be read as the process by which the fragments of modern society can be fused into a dynamic, harmonious totality. At the masked ball, an erotically aroused Haller experiences a mystical unity with individuals who are leading figures in the intellectual life of modern civilization. In the Magic Theater, he gains new insights into both his own psychic development and the German cultural tradition. By implication, Haller, the representative of *Geist*, can use his knowledge to enhance the intellectual life of the people with whom he is mystically joined. Thus, the process of the individual rejuvenation in Hesse's *Steppenwolf* is a model for establishing new and more meaningful cultural relations in modern society.

The cultural crisis is not definitively resolved in *Der Zauberberg*. Castorp does move through the intellectual labyrinth, but he does not find the meaning of life in his discussions with Behrens, Naphta, and Settembrini. In the end, he ventures out alone to the snowy mountaintop, an area of eros and elemental forces of nature. Like Haller, Castorp is drawn by eros into the realm of mystical vision. Castorp effectively enters the collective unconscious of Germany and states his new understanding of life in his interpretation of the dream. Castorp's interpretation amounts to a restatement of Mann's notion of humanity. If Schopenhauer's philosophy is applied to humanity, then it can easily be seen that the idea of the body underlies the idea of community in humanity. Thus, Castorp's interpretation of life belongs within the framework of idealist aesthetics; emotive or sensuous bonds (*Liebe*) link the individual to the community. But it is this relationship between the individual and the community which is problematized in *Der Zauberberg*. Unlike Haller, Castorp does not experience a feeling of mystical unity with the other figures in the text. Further, although he has an intellectual breakthrough by entering the collective unconscious, there seems to be little chance of using his insights to enhance the intellectual life of society. The war labyrinth, the recurrence of the sanatorium labyrinth, indicates that the cultural crisis results in the First World War, a cataclysmic political catastrophe. In *Der Zauberberg*, the political crisis marks the definitive politicization of the realm of the body, which of course defines the relationship of the individual to the community. In this context, Castorp's appearance in the war labyrinth has several possible meanings. I would argue that Castorp learns how to understand cultural forces on the mountain, and he is now challenged to find a political form of humanity to save civilization from the politically diseased sympathy with death.

The variations of the motif of the labyrinth in the three texts testify to the complexity of the cultural crisis. It is true that the individual questers in *Der Steppenwolf* and *Der Zauberberg* show how individuals can find intellectual and existential orientation. But many of Mann's contemporaries did not engage in political reflection and therefore remained intellectually disoriented, much like the conservative professor in Hesse's *Steppenwolf*. Their adherence to older, petrified notions of the cultural tradition made them susceptible to the political form of disease.

Notes

Notes to Chapter 1

1. Max von Brück, "Das Labyrinth," *Die Wandlung* 2 (1947): 295-308.

2. Terry Eagleton, *The Ideology of the Aesthetic*, (Cambridge, Mass: Basil Blackwell, 1990). Eagleton points out how German Idealism deals with various notions of corporality, but he goes too far in stressing the centrality of the body in post-Enlightenment thinking.

3. Using Eagleton as a starting point, I will refer to the broader philosophical and cultural tradition that begins in German Idealism as idealist aesthetics. I will refer to the literary tradition which was decisively shaped by German Idealism as the Classical and Romantic tradition.

4. In the analyses which I cite in this study, there are no references to literary labyrinths in the eighteenth century.

5. See Manfred Schmeling, *Der labyrinthische Diskurs. Vom Mythos zum Erzählmodell* (Frankfort on the Main: Athenäum, 1987), and Horst S. and Ingrid Daemmrich, *Themen und Motive in der Literatur* (Tübingen: Francke, 1987) 206-207.

6. See Reinhart Koselleck, *Futures Past: The Semantics of Time*, trans. Keith Tribe (Cambridge: MIT P, 1985) 267-288.

7. Malcolm Bradbury and James McFarlane, "Cultural and Intellectual Climate of Modernism," *Modernism. A Guide to European Literature 1890-1930*, ed. Malcolm Bradbury and James McFarlane (New York: Penguin, 1976) 57.

8. Schmeling does examine the labyrinth as a metaphor in Kafka's *Schloß*, but does not analyze city labyrinths in modernist German literature. I will consider Schmeling's views in my interpretation of Kafka's *Prozeß* in chapter 3.

9. See Dietrich Scheunemann, *Romankrise. Die Entstehungs-geschichte der modernen Romanpoetik in Deutschland*, Medium Literatur 2 (Heidelberg: Quelle and Meyer, 1978).

10. Russell Berman, *The Rise of the Modern German Novel* (Cambridge Mass.: Harvard U P, 1986).

11. Franz Kafka, *Der Prozeß*, *Gesammelte Werke*, 11 vols. ed. Max Brod, Fischer Lizenzausgabe (Frankfort on the Main: Fischer, 1950-1974).

12. Hermann Hesse, *Der Steppenwolf*, *Gesammelte Werke*, 12 vols. (Frankfort on the Main: Suhrkamp, 1970). 7: 181-413. Future references to

this edition will be abbreviated *SW*.

13. Thomas Mann, *Der Zauberberg, Gesammelte Werke*, 13 vols. (Frankfort on the Main: Fischer, 1960). vol. 3. All citations from Mann's works are from this edition. Future references to the Fischer edition will be abbreviated *GW*.

14. See Arthur Schopenhauer, *The World as Will and Representation*, trans. E. F. J. Payne, 2 vols. (New York: Dover, 1966).

15. Friedrich Nietzsche, *The Gay Science*, trans. Walter Kaufmann (New York: Random House, 1974).

16. See Eric Blondel, *Nietzsche: The Body and Culture*, trans. Seán Hand (Stanford, Calif.: Stanford U P, 1991).

17. Friedrich Nietzsche, *The Will to Power*, trans. Walter Kaufmann and R. J. Hollingdale (New York: Vintage Books, 1967).

18. Friedrich Nietzsche, "The Birth of Tragedy," *The Birth of Tragedy and the Case of Wagner*, trans. Walter Kaufmann (New York: Vintage Books, 1967) 15-144.

19. Martin Heidegger, *Being and Time*, trans. John Macquarrie and Edward Robinson (New York: Harper & Collins, 1962). Future references to this text will be abbreviated *BT*.

20. See also Didier Franck, *Heidegger et le Problème de l'espace* (Paris: Minuit, 1986) 90-98.

21. Martin Heidegger, *Kant and the Problem of Metaphysics,* ed. and trans. Richard Taft (Bloomington Ind.: Indiana U P, 1990). References to this text will be abbreviated *KPM*.

22. Charles Sherover, *Heidegger, Kant and Time* (Bloomington: Indiana U P, 1971) 163.

23. Gustav René Hocke, *Manierismus in der Literatur* (Reinbek: Rowohlt, 1959) 230.

Notes to Chapter 2

1. Umberto Eco, *Semiotics and the Philosophy of Language* (Bloomington, Ind.: Indiana U P, 1984).

2. Penelope Reed Doob, *The Idea of the Labyrinth from Classical Antiquity through the Middle Ages* (Ithaca: Cornell U P, 1990) 18.

3. C. N. Deedes, "The Labyrinth," *The Labyrinth: Further Studies in the Relation between Myth and Ritual in the Ancient World*, ed. S. H. Hooke (New York: MacMillan, 1935) 3-42.

4. R. F. Willetts, *The Civilization of Ancient Crete* (London: Batsford, 1977).

5. Donald A. MacKenzie, *Myths of Crete and Pre-Hellenic Europe* (1918; Boston: Longwood, 1977) 177.

6. Karoly Kerenyi, *Labyrinth Studien* (Zurich: Rhein, 1959).

7. Hermann Kern, "Image of the World and Sacred Realm. Labyrinth-Cities-City-Labyrinths," *Daidalos* 3 (March 15, 1982): 19.

8. Gerald Gillespie, *Garden and Labyrinth of Time*, German Studies in America 56 (New York: Peter Lang, 1988).

9. Wendy Faris, *Labyrinths of Language. Symbolic Landscapes and Narrative Design in Modern Fiction* (Baltimore: Johns Hopkins U P, 1988).

10. See also Werner Senn, "The labyrinth image in verbal art: sign, symbol, icon?" *Word and Image* 3 (1986): 219-230.

Notes to Chapter 3

1. Gilles Deleuze and Felix Guattari, *Kafka: Toward a Minor Literature*, trans. Dana Polan, Theory and History of Literature 30 (Minneapolis: U of Minnesota P, 1986).

2. Hermann Pongs, *Franz Kafka, Dichter des Labyrinths* (Heidelberg: Rothe, 1960).

3. Franz Kafka, *Der Prozeß*, *Gesammelte Werke* ed. Max Brod (Frankfort on the Main: Fischer, 1953). I will cite the text as *Der Prozeß* in quotations.

4. Wilhelm Emrich, *Franz Kafka*, 2nd ed. (Frankfort on the Main: Athenäum, 1960) 292-293.

5. Walter H. Sokel, *Franz Kafka. Tragik und Ironie* (Munich and Vienna: Albert Langen-Georg Muller, 1964) 154.

6. Horst Turk, "betrügen...ohne Betrug. Das Problem der literarischen Legitimation am Beispiel Kafkas," *Urszenen. Literaturewissenschaft als Diskursanalyse und Diskurskritik*, ed. Friedrich Kittler and Horst Turk (Frankfort on the Main: Suhrkamp, 1977) 381-407.

7. Ulf Eisele, *Die Struktur des modernen deutschen Romans* (Tübingen: Niemeyer, 1984) 324-325.

8. Avital Ronell, "Doing Kafka in *The Castle*: A Poetics of Desire," *Kafka and The Contemporary Critical Performance*, ed. Alan Udoff (Bloomington, Ind.: Indiana U P, 1987) 214-235.

9. Gerhard Neumann, "Nachrichten vom 'Pontus.' Das Problem der Kunst im Werke Franz Kafkas," *Schriftverkehr*, ed. Wolf Kittler and Gerhard

Neumann (Freiburg: Rombach, 1990) 164-198.

10. For an excellent survey of poststructuralist readings of Kafka, see Rolf J. Goebel, "Kafka, der Poststrukturalismus und die Geschichte," *Studies in Language and Culture* 15 (1989): 199-224.

11. Clayton Koelb, *Kafka's Rhetoric. The Passion of Reading* (Ithaca: Cornell U P, 1989) 10.

12. Henry Sussman, *Franz Kafka: Geometrician of the Metaphor* (Madison, Wisconsin: Coda, 1978) 101.

13. Stanley Corngold, *Franz Kafka. The Necessity of Form* (Ithaca: Cornell U P, 1988).

14. Rainer Nägele, "Kafka and Interpretative Desire," *Kafka and The Contemporary Critical Performance*, ed. Alan Udoff (Bloomington and Indianapolis: Indiana U P, 1987) 16-29.

15. Jacques Derrida, "Devant la loi," trans. Avitall Ronell, *Kafka and The Contemporary Critical Performance*, ed. Alan Udoff (Bloomington and Indianapolis: Indiana U P, 1987) 141.

16. Franz Kafka, "Betrachtungen über Sünde, Leid, Hoffnung und den wahren Weg," *Hochzeitsvorbereitungen auf dem Lande und andere Prosa aus dem Nachlaß, Gesammelte Werke*, ed. Max Brod (Frankfort on the Main: Fischer, 1953) 40.

17. Gustav Janouch, *Gespräche mit Kafka* (Frankfort on the Main: Fischer, 1968) 140.

18. Franz Kafka, "Forschungen eines Hundes," *Beschreibung eines Kampfes, Gesammelte Werke*, ed. Max Brod (Frankfort on the Main: Fischer, 1954) 240-290. I will cite volume as *Beschreibung*.

19. Franz Kafka, *Tagebücher* 1910-1923, *Gesammelte Werke*, ed. Max Brod (Frankfort on the Main: Fischer, 1967) 320-321.

20. Irving Howe, *The Critical Point on Literature and Culture* (New York: Horizon, 1973) 42.

21. Volker Klotz, *Die erzählte Stadt. Ein Sujet als Herausforderung des Romans von Lesage bis Döblin* (Munich: Hanser, 1969) 145.

22. Diana Festa-McCormick, *The City as Catalyst* (Rutherford, New Jersey: Farleigh Dickenson U P, 1979).

23. Hartwig Isernhagen, "Die Bewußtseinskrise der Moderne und die Erfahrung der Stadt als Labyrinth," *Die Stadt in der Literatur*, ed. Cord Meckseper and Elisabeth Schraut (Göttingen: Vandenhoeck und Ruprecht, 1983) 81-104.

24. Heidrun Suhr, "Die fremde Stadt. Über Geschichte von Aufstieg und

Untergang in der Metropole," *In der großen Stadt, Die Metropole als kulturtheoretische Kategorie*, ed. Thomas Steinfeld and Heidrun Suhr, Athenäums Monographien Literaturwissenschaft 101 (Frankfort on the Main: Hain, 1990) 27.

25. See also Christoph Bezzel, *Natur bei Kafka*, Erlanger Beiträge zur Sprach- und Kunstwissenschaft 15 (Nuremberg: Carl, 1963) 88-92.

26. Axel Dornemann, *Im Labyrinth der Bürokratie* (Heidelberg: Carl Winter, 1984).

27. Bettina Küter, *Mehr Raum als sonst. Zum Gelebten Raum im Werk Franz Kafka*, Reihe 1, Deutsche Sprache und Literatur 1154 (Frankfort on the Main: Peter Lang, 1989) 176-178.

28. Jacob and Wilhelm Grimm. *Deutsches Wörterbuch*, 1st ed. 16 vols. (Leipzig: Hirzel, 1854-1954) 6: 535.

29. Franz Kafka, *Das Schloß, Gesammelte Werke*, ed. Max Brod, Fischer Lizenzausgabe (Frankfort on the Main: Fischer, 1955).

30. Heinz Politzer, *Franz Kafka. Parable and Paradox* (Ithaca: Cornell U P, 1958) 172.

31. Gerhard Kaiser, "Franz Kafkas *Prozeß*: Versuch einer Interpretation," *Euphorion* 52 (1958): 44.

32. Helmut Richter, *Franz Kafka. Werk und Entwurf* (Berlin (GDR): Rütten and Loening, 1962) 198-199.

33. Jacques Lacan, "Aggressivity in Psychoanalysis," *Écrits*, trans. Alan Sheridan (New York: Norton, 1977) 8-29.

34. Georg Lukács, *History and Class Consciousness*, trans. Rodney Livingstone (Cambridge, Mass.: MIT U P, 1971) 87.

35. Josef Hermann Mense, *Die Bedeutung des Todes im Werk Franz Kafkas*, diss., Gesamthochschule Kassel, 1978, Kasseler Arbeiten zur Sprache und Literatur 4 (Frankfort on the Main: Peter Lang, 1978) 80.

36. Jürg Beat Honegger, *Das Phänomen der Angst bei Franz Kafka*, Philologische Studien und Quellen 81 (West Berlin: Erich Schmidt, 1975) 267.

37. Thomas Anz, "Der schöne und der häßliche Tod," *Klassik und Moderne*, ed. Karl Richter and Jörg Schönert (Stuttgart: Metzler, 1983) 418. Future references to this essay will be abbreviated *SHT*.

38. Thomas Anz, "Die Historizität der Angst," *Jahrbuch der deutschen Schillergesellschaft* 19 (1975): 274. References to this essay will be abbreviated *HdA*.

39. Dieter Claessens, "Über gesellschaftlichen Druck, Angst und Furcht," *Die politische und gesellschaftliche Rolle der Angst*, ed. Heinz Wiesbrock

(Frankfort on the Main: Europäische Verlagsanstalt, 1967) 141.

40. Fritz Billeter, *Das Dichterische bei Kafka und Kierkegaard*, diss., U of Basel 1965 (Winterthur: Keller, 1965) 114.

Notes to Chapter 4

1. Joseph Mileck, *Hermann Hesse: Life and Art* (Berkeley: U of California P, 1978) 177.

2. Colin Wilson, "Outsider und Bürger," *Materialien zu Hermann Hesses 'Der Steppenwolf,'* ed. Volker Michels (Frankfort on the Main: Suhrkamp, 1972) 309-317.

3. Claude Hill, "Hermann Hesse als Kritiker der bürgerlichen Zivilisation," *Monatshefte* 40 (1948): 241-253.

4. George W. Field, *Hermann Hesse*, Twayne World Author Series 93 Germany (Boston: Twayne, 1970) 94-95.

5. Margot Böttcher, "Der einsame Citoyen: Hermann Hesses Verhältnis zum Bürgertum," *Neue Deutsche Literatur* 5 (1952): 7-19.

6. Emmanuel Maier, "The Psychology of C. G. Jung in the Works of Hermann Hesse," diss., New York U, 1952.

7. Ludwig Völker, "Zwischen Figur und Person: die Gestalt der Hermine in Hesses *Steppenwolf*," *Etudes Germaniques* 25 (January-March 1970): 41-50.

8. Edward Timms, "Hesse's Therapeutic Fiction," *Modernism and the European Unconscious*, ed, Peter Collier and Judy Davies (New York: St. Martin's, 1988) 165-184.

9. See also David Artiss, "Schlüsselsymbole in Hesses *Steppenwolf*," *Seminar* 7 (1971): 85-101.

10. Eugen Stelzig, *Hermann Hesse's Fictions of the Self: The Confessional Autobiography* (Princeton: Princeton U P, 1988) 216.

11. M. L. von Franz, "The Process of Individuation." *Man and his Symbols*. ed. Carl G. Jung (New York: Dell, 1968) 157-254.

12. Carl Gustav Jung, *Psychological Types*, trans. H. Godwin Baynes (New York: Harcourt, Brace & Co., 1923) 593.

13. Fränzi Maierhöfer, "Die unbewältigte Stadt. Zum Problem der Urbanisation in der Literatur," *Stimmen der Zeit* 187 (January-June 1971) 310.

14. See also Astrid Khera, *Hermann Hesses Romane der Krisenzeit*, Abhandlungen zur Kunst-, Musik-, und Literaturwissenschaft 253 (Bonn: Bouvier, 1978) 163.

15. Hermann Hesse, *Demian, Gesammelte Werke,* 12 vols. (Frankfort on

the Main: Suhrkamp, 1970). vol. 5: 5-163.

16. Theodore Ziolkowski, *The Novels of Hermann Hesse. A Study in Theme and Structure* (Princeton: Princeton U P, 1974) 189. Ziolkowski's groundbreaking study is still the most influential work on Hesse to date.

17. Hermann Hesse, "Gedanken zu Dostojewskys *Idiot*," *Materialien zu Hermann Hesses 'Der Steppenwolf,'* ed. Volker Michels (Frankfort on the Main: Suhrkamp, 1972) 217-223. Future references to this text will be abbreviated *GDI*.

18. Paul Kluckhohn, *Die Auffassung der Liebe in der Literatur des 18. Jahrhunderts und in der Romantik* (Tübingen: Niemeyer, 1966) 454.

19. Donald Nelson, *Portrait of the Artist as Hermes,* University of North Carolina Studies in the Germanic Languages and Literatures 70 (Chapel Hill, North Carolina: U of North Carolina P, 1970) 76.

20. Anders Nygren, *Agape and Eros*, trans. Philip S. Watson (London: S. P. C. K., 1953) 493.

21. Hans Lüthi, *Hermann Hesse. Natur und Geist*, Sprache und Literatur 61 (Stuttgart: Kohlhammer, 1970) 86.

22. Mark Boulby, *Hermann Hesse. His Mind and Art* (Ithaca: Cornell U P, 1967) 200.

23. Joseph L. Henderson, "Ancient Myths and Modern Man," *Man and His Symbols*, ed. Carl Gustav Jung (New York: Dell, 1968) 117.

Notes to Chapter 5

1. Thomas Mann, *Der Tod in Venedig, GW* 8: 444-525.

2. Helmut Koopmann, "Die Kategorie des Hermetischen in Thomas Manns Roman *Der Zauberberg*," *Zeitschrift für deutsche Philologie* 80 (1961) 407.

3. Thomas Mann, *Betrachtungen eines Unpolitischen, GW* 12: 9-598.

4. Thomas Mann, "Von deutscher Republik," *GW* 11: 809-852.

5. Thomas Mann, "Geist und Wesen der Republik," *GW* 11: 854.

6. Thomas Mann, "Goethe und Tolstoi," *GW* 9: 124.

7. Thomas Mann, "Schopenhauer," *GW* 9: 528-580.

8. Erich Heller, *The Ironic German. A Study of Thomas Mann* (Boston: Atlantic-Little and Brown, 1958).

9. Manfred Dierks, *Studien zu Mythos und Psychologie bei Thomas Mann*. Thomas Mann Studien 2 (Berne: Francke, 1972) 56.

10. See also Francis Bulhof, *Transpersonalismus und Synchronizität.*

Wiederholung als Strukturmerkmal in Thomas Manns 'Zauberberg,' diss., U of Groningen, 1966 (Groningen: Denderen, 1966) 42.

11. Géza von Molnár, *Romantic Vision, Ethical Context. Novalis and Artistic Autonomy*, Theory and History of Literature 39 (Minneapolis: U of Minnesota P, 1987).

12. Thomas Mann, "Pariser Rechenschaft," *GW* 11: 9-97.

13. See Hermann J. Weigand, *Thomas Mann's Novel 'Der Zauberberg'. A Study* (1933. New York: AMS, 1971) 142 and T. J. Reed, *Thomas Mann. The Uses of Tradition* (Oxford: Clarendon, 1974) 294.

14. See also Fritz Kaufmann, *The World as Will and Representation* (Boston: Beacon, 1959) 57.

15. Heinz Saueressig, *Die Bildwelt von Hans Castorps Frosttraum* (Biberach: Thomae, 1967) 2-13.

16. Herbert Lehnert, "Hans Castorps Vision: Eine Studie zum Aufbau von Thomas Manns Roman *Der Zauberberg*," *The Rice Institute Pamphlet* 47 (April 1960): 1-37.

17. See also Erika A. Wirtz, "Zitat und Leitmotiv bei Thomas Mann," *German Life and Letters* 7 (1954): 129.

18. Peter Pütz, "Thomas Mann und Nietzsche," *Thomas Mann und die Tradition*, ed. Peter Pütz (Frankfort on the Main: Athenäum, 1971) 239.

19. Ludwig Uhlig, *Der Todesgenius in der deutschen Literatur,* Untersuchungen zur deutschen Literaturgeschichte 12 (Tübingen: Niemeyer, 1975) 5-35, 104-109.

20. E. M. Butler, *The Tyranny of Greece over Germany* (Boston: Beacon, 1958).

21. Peter Heller, *Dialectics and Nihilism. Essays on Lessing, Nietzsche, Mann and Kafka* (Amherst: U of Massachusetts P, 1966) 162.

22. Helmut Koopmann is one of the few critics who argues that Mann embraces Enlightenment. See Helmut Koopmann, *Der klassich-moderne Roman in Deutschland*, Sprache und Literatur 113 (Stuttgart: Kohlhammer, 1983). I will cite this text as *KMR*

23. Børge Kristiansen, *Thomas Manns 'Zauberberg' und Schopenhauers Metaphysik.* 2nd ed. Studien zur Literatur der Moderne 10 (Bonn: Bouvier, 1986) 224.

24. See Hans Wisskirchen, *Zeitgeschichte im Roman. Zu Thomas Manns "Zauberberg" und "Doktor Faustus,"* Thomas Mann Studien 6 (Berlin: Francke, 1986) 90-97.

25. See also Helmut Gutmann, "Das Musikkapital in Thomas Manns

Zauberberg," *German Quarterly* 47 (1974): 423.

26. To my knowledge, T. J. Reed is the only critic who has made this point (245).

27. Thomas Mann, "Vorspruch zu einer musikalischen Nietzsche-Feier," *GW* 10: 180-184.

28. See also Gutmann (424), and Hans Wysling, "*Der Zauberberg.*" *Thomas Mann-Handbuch*, ed. Helmut Koopmann (Stuttgart: Kröner, 1990) 419.

29. Hans Mayer, *Thomas Mann* (Frankfort on the Main: Suhrkamp, 1980) 131.

Notes to Chapter 6

1. See George Mosse, *The Crisis of German Ideology* (New York: Grosset & Dunlap, 1964).

Works Cited

Anz, Thomas. "Der schöne und der häßliche Tod." *Klassik und Moderne*. Ed. Karl Richter and Jörg Schönert. Stuttgart: Metzler, 1983. 409-432.

__. "Die Historizität der Angst." *Jahrbuch der deutschen Schillergesellschaft* 19 (1975): 237-283.

Artiss, David. "Schlüsselsymbole in Hesses *Steppenwolf.*" *Seminar* 7 (1971): 85-101.

Berman, Russell. *The Rise of the Modern German Novel*. Cambridge Mass.: Harvard U P, 1986.

Bezzel, Christoph. *Natur bei Kafka*. Erlanger Beiträge zur Sprach- und Kunstwissenschaft 15. Nuremberg: Carl, 1963.

Billeter, Fritz. *Das Dichterische bei Kafka und Kierkegaard*. Diss. U of Basel. Winterthur: Keller, 1965.

Blondel, Eric. *Nietzsche: The Body and Culture*. Trans. Seán Hand. Stanford, Calif.: Stanford U P, 1991.

Böttcher, Margot. "Der einsame Citoyen: Hermann Hesses Verhältnis zum Bürgertum." *Neue Deutsche Literatur* 5 (1957): 7-19.

Boulby, Mark. *Hermann Hesse. His Mind and Art*. Ithaca: Cornell U P, 1967.

Bradbury, Malcolm and James McFarlane. "Cultural and Intellectual Climate of Modernism." *Modernism. A Guide to European Literature 1890-1930*. Ed. Malcolm Bradbury and James McFarlane. New York: Penguin, 1976. 57.

Brück, Max von. "Das Labyrinth." *Die Wandlung* 2 (1947): 295-308.

Bulhof, Francis. *Transpersonalismus und Synchronizität. Wiederholung als Strukturmerkmal in Thomas Manns 'Zauberberg'*. Diss. U of Groningen, 1966. Groningen: Denderen, 1966.

136

Butler, E. M. *The Tyranny of Greece over Germany*. Boston: Beacon, 1958.

Claessens, Dieter. "Über gesellschaftlichen Druck, Angst und Furcht." *Die politische und gesellschaftliche Rolle der Angst*. Ed. Heinz Wiesbrock. Frankfort on the Main: Europäische Verlagsanstalt, 1967. 135-150.

Corngold, Stanley. *The Necessity of Form*. Ithaca: Cornell U P, 1988.

Daemmrich, Horst and Ingrid. *Themen and Motive in der Literatur*. Tübingen: Francke, 1987.

Deedes, C. N. "The Labyrinth." *The Labyrinth: Further Studies in the Relation between Myth and Ritual in the Ancient World*. Ed. S. H. Hooke. New York: MacMillan, 1935. 3-42.

Deleuze, Gilles and Felix Guattari. *Kafka: Toward A Minor Literature*. Trans. Dana Polan. Theory and History of Literature 30. Minneapolis: U of Minnesota P, 1986.

Derrida, Jacques. "Devant la loi." Trans. Avitall Ronell. *Kafka and the Contemporary Performance*. Ed. Alan Udoff. Bloomington: Indiana U P, 1987. 128-149.

Dierks, Manfred. *Studien zu Mythos und Psychologie bei Thomas Mann*. Thomas Mann Studien 2. Berne: Francke, 1972.

Doob, Penelope Reed. *The Idea of the Labyrinth from Classical Antiquity through the Middle Ages*. Ithaca: Cornell U P, 1990.

Dornemann, Axel. *Im Labyrinth der Bürokratie*. Heidelberg: Carl Winter, 1984.

Eagleton, Terry. *The Ideology of the Aesthetic*. Cambridge, Mass: Basil Blackwell, 1990.

Eco, Umberto. *Semiotics and the Philosophy of Language*. Bloomington, Ind.: Indiana U P, 1984.

Eisele, Ulf. *Die Struktur des modernen deutschen Romans*. Tübingen: Niemeyer, 1984.

Emrich, Wilhelm. *Franz Kafka*. 2nd Ed. Frankfort on the Main: Athenäum, 1960.

Faris, Wendy B. *Labyrinths of Language. Symbolic Landscape and Narrative Design in Modern Fiction*. Baltimore: Johns Hopkins U P, 1988.

Festa-McCormick, Diana. *The City as Catalyst*. Rutherford, New Jersey: Farleigh Dickenson U P, 1979.

Field, George. W. *Hermann Hesse*. Twayne World Author Series 93 Germany. Boston: Twayne, 1970.

Franck, Didier. *Heidegger et le Problème de l'espace*. Paris: Minuit, 1986.

Franz, M. L, von. "The Process of Individuation." *Man and His Symbols*. Ed. Carl G. Jung. 21st ed. New York: Dell, 1968. 157-254.

Gillespie, Gerald. *Garden and Labyrinth of Time*. German Studies in America 56. New York: Peter Lang, 1988.

Goebel, Rolf J. "Kafka, der Poststrukturalismus und die Geschichte." *Studies in Language and Culture*. 15 (1989): 199-224.

Grimm, Jacob and Wilhelm. *Deutsches Wörterbuch*. 16 vols. Leipzig: Hirzel, 1854-1954.

Gutmann, Helmut. "Das Musikkapital in Thomas Manns *Zauberberg*." *German Quarterly* 47 (1974): 415-431.

Heidegger, Martin. *Being and Time*. Trans. John Macquarrie and Edward Robinson. New York: Harper & Collins, 1962.

__. *Kant and the Problem of Metaphysics*. Ed. and trans. Richard Taft. Bloomington Ind.: Indiana U P, 1990.

Heller, Erich. *The Ironic German. A Study of Thomas Mann*. Boston: Atlantic-Little and Brown, 1958.

Heller, Peter. *Dialectics and Nihilism. Essays on Lessing, Nietzsche, Mann and Kafka*. Amherst: U of Massachusetts P, 1966.

Henderson, Joseph, L. "Ancient Myths and Modern Man." *Man and His Symbols*. Ed. Carl G. Jung. New York: Dell, 1968. 95-156.

Hesse, Hermann. "Gedanken zu Dostojewskys *Idiot*." *Materialien zu Hermann Hesses 'Der Steppenwolf.'* Ed. Volker Michels. Frankfort on the Main: Suhrkamp, 1972. 217-223.

Hesse, Hermann. *Gesammelte Werke*. 12 vols. Frankfort on the Main: Suhrkamp, 1970.

Hill, Claude. "Hermann Hesse als Kritiker der bürgerlichen Zivilisation." *Monatshefte* 40 (1948): 241-253.

Hocke, Gustav René. *Manierismus in der Literatur*. Reinbek: Rowohlt, 1959.

Honnegger, Jürg Beat. *Das Phänomen der Angst bei Franz Kafka*. Philologische Studien und Quellen 81. West Berlin: Erich Schmidt, 1975.

Howe, Irving. *The Critical Point on Literature and Culture*. New York: Horizon, 1973.

Isernhagen, Hartwig. "Die Bewußtseinskrise der Moderne und die Erfahrung der Stadt als Labyrinth." *Die Stadt in der Literatur*. Ed. Cord Meckseper and Elisabeth Schraut. Göttingen: Vandenhoeck und Ruprecht, 1983. 81-104.

Janouch, Gustav. *Gespräche mit Kafka*. Frankfort on the Main: Fischer, 1968.

Jung, Carl Gustav. *Psychological Types*. Trans. H. Godwin Baynes. New York: Harcourt, Brace & Co., 1923.

Kafka, Franz. *Gesammelte Werke.* Ed. Max Brod. 11 vols. Fischer Lizenzausgabe. Frankfort on the Main: Fischer, 1950-1974.

Kaiser, Gerhard. "Franz Kafkas 'Prozeß': Versuch einer Interpretation." *Euphorion* 52 (1958): 23-49.

Kaufmann, Fritz. *The World as Will and Representation.* Boston: Beacon, 1959.

Kehra, Astrid. *Hermann Hesses Romane der Krisenzeit.* Abhandlungen zur Kunst-, Musik- und Literaturwissenschaft 253. Bonn: Bouvier, 1978.

Kerenyi, Karoly. *Labyrinth Studien.* Zurich: Rhein, 1959.

Kern, Hermann. "Image of the World and Sacred Realm. Labyrinth-Cities-City-Labyrinths." *Daidalos* 3 (March 15, 1982): 10-25.

Klotz, Volker. *Die erzählte Stadt. Ein Sujet als Herausforderung des Romans von Lesage bis Döblin.* Munich: Hanser, 1969.

Kluckhohn, Paul. *Die Auffassung der Liebe in der Literatur des 18. Jahrhunderts und in der deutschen Romantik.* Tübingen: Niemeyer, 1966.

Koelb, Clayton. *Kafka's Rhetoric. The Passion of Reading.* Ithaca: Cornell U P, 1989.

Koopmann, Helmut. "Die Kategorie des Hermetischen in Thomas Manns Roman *Der Zauberberg.*" *Zeitschrift für deutsche Philologie* 80 (1961): 404-422.

__. *Der klassich-moderne Roman in Deutschland.* Sprache und Literatur 113. Stuttgart: Kohlhammer, 1983.

Koselleck, Reinhart. *Futures Past: The Semantics of Time.* Trans. Keith Tribe. Cambridge: MIT P, 1985.

140

Kristiansen, Børge. *Thomas Manns 'Zauberberg' und Schopenhauers Metaphysik*. 2nd ed. Studien zur Literatur der Moderne 10. Bonn: Bouvier, 1986.

Küter, Bettina. *Mehr Raum als sonst. Zum Gelebten Raum im Werk Franz Kafka*. Reihe 1, Deutsche Sprache und Literatur 1154. Frankfort on the Main: Peter Lang, 1989.

Lacan, Jacques. "Aggressivity in Psychoanalysis." *Écrits*. Trans. Alan Sheridan. New York: Norton, 1977. 8-29.

Lehnert, Herbert. "Hans Castorps Vision: Eine Studie zum Aufbau von Thomas Manns Roman *Der Zauberberg*." *The Rice Institute Pamphlet* 47 (April 1960): 1-37.

Lüthi, Hans. *Hermann Hesse. Natur und Geist*. Sprache und Literatur 61. Stuttgart: Kohlhammer, 1970.

Lukács, Georg. *History and Class Consciousness*. Trans. Rodney Livingstone. Cambridge, Mass.: MIT U P, 1971.

MacKenzie, Donald A. *Myths of Crete and Pre-Hellenic Europe*. 1918. Boston: Longwood, 1977.

Maier, Emanuel. "The Psychology of C. G. Jung in the Works of Hermann Hesse." Diss. New York U, 1952.

Maierhöfer, Fränzi. "Die unbewältigte Stadt. Zum Problem der Urbanisation in der Literatur." *Stimmen der Zeit* 187 (January-June 1971): 309-325.

Mann, Thomas. *Gesammelte Werke*. 13 vols. Frankfort on the Main: Fischer, 1960.

Mayer, Hans. *Thomas Mann*. Frankfort on the Main: Suhrkamp, 1980.

Mense, Josef Hermann. *Die Bedeutung des Todes im Werk Franz Kafkas*. Diss. Gesamthochschule Kassel, 1978. Kasseler Arbeiten zur Sprache und Literatur 4. Frankfort on the Main: Peter Lang, 1978.

Mileck, Joseph. *Hermann Hesse: Life and Art*. Berkeley: U of California P, 1978.

Molnár, Géza, von. *Romantic Vision, Ethical Context. Novalis and Artistic Autonomy*. Theory and History of Literature 39. Minneapolis: U of Minnesota Press, 1987.

Mosse, George. *The Crisis of German Ideology*. New York: Grosset & Dunlap, 1964.

Nägele, Rainer. "Kafka and Interpretative Desire." *Kafka and The Contemporary Critical Performance*. Ed. Alan Udoff. Bloomington and Indianapolis: Indiana U P, 1987. 16-29.

Nelson, Donald. *Portrait of the Artist as Hermes*. University of North Carolina Studies in the Germanic Languages and Literatures 70. Chapel Hill, North Carolina: U of North Carolina P, 1970.

Neumann, Gerhard. "Nachrichten vom 'Pontus.' Das Problem der Kunst im Werke Franz Kafkas." *Schriftverkehr*. Ed. Wolf Kittler and Gerhard Neumann. Freiburg: Rombach, 1990. 164-198.

Nietzsche, Friedrich. "The Birth of Tragedy." *The Birth of Tragedy and the Case of Wagner*. Trans. Walter Kaufmann. New York: Vintage Books, 1967. 15-144.

___. *The Gay Science*. Trans. Walter Kaufmann. New York: Random House, 1974.

___. *The Will to Power*. Trans. Walter Kaufmann and R. J. Hollingdale. New York: Vintage Books, 1967.

Nygren, Anders. *Agape and Eros*. Trans. Philip S. Watson. London: S. P. C. K., 1953.

Politzer, Heinz. *Franz Kafka. Parable and Paradox*. Ithaca: Cornell U P, 1958.

Pongs, Hermann. *Franz Kafka, Dichter des Labyrinths*. Heidelberg: Rothe, 1960.

Pütz, Peter. "Thomas Mann und Nietzsche." *Thomas Mann und die Tradition*. Ed. Peter Pütz. Frankfort on the Main: Athenäum, 1971. 225-249.

Reed, T. J. *Thomas Mann. The Uses of Tradition*. Oxford: Clarendon, 1974.

Richter, Helmut. *Franz Kafka. Werk und Entwurf*. East Berlin: Rütten and Loening, 1962.

Ronell, Avital. "Doing Kafka in *The Castle*: A Poetics of Desire." *Kafka and The Contemporary Critical Performance*. Ed. Alan Udoff. Bloomington, Ind.: Indiana U P, 1987. 214-235.

Sauereßig, Heinz. *Die Bildwelt von Hans Castorps Frosttraum*. Biberach: Thomae, 1967.

Scheunemann, Dietrich. *Romankrise. Die Entstehungsgeschichte der modernen Romanpoetik in Deutschland*. Medium Literatur 2. Heidelberg: Quelle and Meyer, 1978.

Schmeling, Manfred. *Der labyrinthische Diskurs. Vom Mythos zum Erzählmodell*. Frankfort on the Main: Athenäum, 1987.

Schopenhauer, Arthur. *The World as Will and Representation*. Trans. E. F. J. Payne. 2 vols. New York: Dover, 1966.

Senn, Werner. "The labyrinth image in verbal art: sign, symbol, icon?" *Word and Image* 2 (1986): 219-230.

Sherover, Charles. *Heidegger, Kant and Time*. Bloomington, Ind.: Indiana U P, 1971.

Sokel, Walter H. *Franz Kafka. Tragik und Ironie. Zur Struktur seiner Kunst*. Munich: Albert Lange and Georg Muller, 1964.

Stelzig, Eugen. *Hermann Hesse's Fictions of the Self: The Confessional Autobiography*. Princeton, New Jersey: Princeton U P, 1988.

Suhr, Heidrun. "Die fremde Stadt. Über Geschichte von Aufstieg und Untergang in der Metropole." *In der großen Stadt, Die Metropole als kulturtheoretische Kategorie.* Ed. Thomas Steinfeld and Heidrun Suhr. Athenäums Monographien Literaturwissenschaft 101. Frankfort on the Main: Hain, 1990. 23-40.

Sussman, Henry. *Franz Kafka: Geometrician of the Metaphor.* Madison, Wisconsin: Coda, 1978.

Timms, Edward. "Hesse's Therapeutic Fiction." *Modernism and the European Unconscious.* Ed. Peter Collier and Judy Davies. New York: St. Martin's, 1988. 165-184.

Turk, Horst. "betrügen...ohne Betrug. Das Problem der literarischen Legitimation am Beispiel Kafkas." *Urszenen. Literaturewissenschaft als Diskursanalyse und Diskurskritik.* Ed. Friedrich Kittler and Horst Turk. Frankfort on the Main: Suhrkamp, 1977. 381-407.

Uhlig, Ludwig. *Der Todesgenius in der deutschen Literatur.* Untersuchungen zur deutschen Literaturgeschichte 12. Tübingen: Niemeyer, 1975.

Völker, Ludwig. "Zwischen Figur und Person: die Gestalt der Hermine in Hesses *Steppenwolf.*" *Etudes Germaniques* 25 (January-March 1970): 41-50.

Weigand, Hermann J. *Thomas Mann's Novel 'Der Zauberberg.' A Study.* 1933. New York: AMS, 1971.

Willets, R. F. *The Civilization of Ancient Crete.* London: Batsford, 1977

Wilson, Colin. "Outsider und Bürger." *Materialien zu Hermann Hesses 'Der Steppenwolf'.* Ed. Volker Michels. Frankfort on the Main: Suhrkamp, 1972. 309-317.

Wirtz, Erika A. "Zitat und Leitmotiv bei Thomas Mann." *German Life and Letters* 7(1954): 126-136.

Wisskirchen, Hans. *Zeitgeschichte im Roman. Zu Thomas Manns "Zauberberg" und "Doktor Faustus."* Thomas Mann Studien 6. Berlin: Francke, 1986.

Wysling, Hans. "*Der Zauberberg.*" *Thomas Mann-Handbuch*. Ed. Helmut Koopmann. Stuttgart: Kröner, 1990. 397-422.

Ziolkowski, Theodore. *The novels of Hermann Hesse. A Study in Theme and Structure*. Princeton, New Jersey: Princeton U P, 1974.

Index

Studies on Themes and Motifs in Literature

The series is designed to advance the publication of research pertaining to themes and motifs in literature. The studies cover cross-cultural patterns as well as the entire range of national literatures. They trace the development and use of themes and motifs over extended periods, elucidate the significance of specific themes or motifs for the formation of period styles, and analyze the unique structural function of themes and motifs. By examining themes or motifs in the work of an author or period, the studies point to the impulses authors received from literary tradition, the choices made, and the creative transformation of the cultural heritage. The series will include publications of colloquia and theoretical studies that contribute to a greater understanding of literature.